Girvan Academy

Physics

IS FUN ━━━━━━━━━━━━━━━━━━━━━━━

BOOK THREE

Physics
IS FUN

An introductory course for secondary schools in four volumes

BOOK THREE

Jim Jardine, B.Sc., M.Ed., A.Inst.P.

Head of the Physics Department, George Watson's College, Edinburgh

Illustrated by Geoffrey Salter

 Heinemann Educational Books Ltd · LONDON

Heinemann Educational Books Ltd

London Edinburgh Melbourne Toronto Johannesburg Singapore Auckland Ibadan
Hong Kong Nairobi New Delhi

ISBN 0 435 67474 9

Published by Heinemann Educational Books Ltd
48 Charles Street, London W1X 8AH
Printed in Great Britain at the Pitman Press, Bath

Contents

Conversion Factors

	To change British to S.I. units					To change S.I. to British units				
Mass	lb	→	kg	: ×	0·454	kg	→	lb	: ×	2·20
Length	ft	→	m	: ×	0·305	m	→	ft	: ×	3·28
	mi	→	km	: ×	1·61	km	→	mi	: ×	0·621
Speed	ft/s	→	m/s	: ×	0·305	m/s	→	ft/s	: ×	3·28
	mi/h	→	m/s	: ×	0·447	m/s	→	mi/h	: ×	2·24
Acceleration	ft/s^2	→	m/s^2	: ×	0·305	m/s^2	→	ft/s^2	: ×	3·28
Force	pdl	→	N	: ×	0·138	N	→	pdl	: ×	7·23
	lbf	→	N	: ×	4·45	N	→	lbf	: ×	0·225
Pressure	lbf/in^2	→	N/m^2	: ×	6,890	N/m^2	→	lbf/in^2	: ×	$1·45 \times 10^{-4}$
Energy	ft pdl	→	J	: ×	0·042	J	→	ft pdl	: ×	23·7
	ft lbf	→	J	: ×	1·36	J	→	ft lbf	: ×	0·735
	Btu	→	J	: ×	1,055	J	→	Btu	: ×	$9·48 \times 10^{-4}$
Power	h p	→	W	: ×	746	W	→	h p	: ×	$1·34 \times 10^{-3}$

	c.g.s. → S.I.					S.I. → c.g.s.				
Force	dyn	→	N	: ×	10^{-5}	N	→	dyn	: ×	10^5
	gf	→	N	: ×	$9·81 \times 10^{-3}$	N	→	gf	: ×	102
Energy	erg	→	J	: ×	10^{-7}	J	→	erg	: ×	10^7
	cal	→	J	: ×	4·186	J	→	cal	: ×	0·239

Preface

The first two years of this course provided a qualitative introduction to physics. This year's work is much more quantitative, and covers the third year of a secondary school physics course, following the order of the new Scottish physics syllabus (Sections 8 and 9).

This is primarily a pupil's book intended to be used under the direction of a teacher. Some parts, such as chapter 10, are intended mainly for home reading. No pupil, not even the most brilliant future physics specialist, should be expected to work through every experiment and every problem. Alternative experiments are often provided to allow teachers in schools which are short of certain apparatus to use the equipment available. *Demonstrations* and pupil *Experiments* cover the basic course, and optional practical tasks are included as *Projects* and *Practical Puzzles*. *Projects* can be carried out as individual or group experiments in the laboratory if time permits. Many of them can be done at home, and others are suitable for use in science clubs or at open days. *Practical Puzzles* can be considered simply as problems, or they can be used as practical exercises yielding results which can be analysed.

So that this book may be suitable for all third-year pupils, additional material has been included at the end of each chapter under the heading of *Optional Extras*. This additional material will not be needed by O Grade pupils but some of it may be valuable for those who intend to study physics beyond that level. Only the teacher can decide what material is appropriate to his class. He alone can make the necessary selection.

An attempt has been made to provide experimental details for the use of both teacher and pupil. Subscripts indicate suppliers of apparatus, whose names and addresses are given at the back of the book.

SI of relief

It is hardly surprising that *energy* is not regarded by every schoolboy as one of the great unifying principles of physics. Can he be blamed if he does not realise that the same physical quantity can be measured in ergs or ft Lb or ft lbf or ft lb wt or calories or Calories or therms or kilowatt hours or British Thermal Units or joules or electron-volts?

In this book concepts are introduced in terms of every-day units; for example, speed in miles per hour. Once the concept has been established SI units are used. In the *Système International* (SI) the units are the metre, kilogram, second, ampere, degree Kelvin and candela. Problems will be set in SI units or, in a very few cases, the necessary conversion factor given.

Recommendations of the British Standards Institution have been accepted for the abbreviations used throughout. Roman letters are used for unit abbreviations (e.g. g for grams) and italics for other symbols (e.g. *g* for gravity). As s is used for *seconds* and for *specific heat*, *d* is recommended for *displacement* at O Grade. There is the admitted disadvantage that should a pupil wish to differentiate displacement with respect to time another letter would be preferable. This will, of course, affect only those proceeding to advanced work, and as *l, r, s, x, y* and *z* are then commonly used for displacements this disadvantage is slight. There have, however, been so many requests for retention of *s* that duplicate equations are printed in the margin.

Change of temperature, degC, has now been replaced by °C.

Yesterday, Today and Forever

The physicist, like the theologian, looks for stability in a changing world. He selects those things which remain the same and labels them. Galileo found $\Delta v/\Delta t$ constant for a falling body and so defined acceleration. Moments, momentum and energy are other examples. Each of Newton's laws depends on something remaining the same: v, F/ma and mv.

The theme, then, of this book is *conservation*. Without it, accurate predictions could not be made and scientific thinking would be impossible.

Thanks

I am indebted to several firms and individuals for allowing their photographs to be reproduced.

This book has been produced with the co-operation and encouragement of so many people that I find it impossible adequately to express my thanks for all the help received. Friends and colleagues from the physics departments of several schools and colleges read the manuscript and made many helpful comments and criticisms.

I am particularly grateful to our lab. technician for making and often designing prototype apparatus, to the artist for his amazing patience and skill in interpreting the spirit of the new syllabus and to the publishers for their enthusiasm and guidance throughout the undertaking.

The entire manuscript was read and criticised by Dr Davidson of Aberdeen University. For the time and trouble he so willingly took I should like to express my sincere thanks.

Edinburgh, September 1965   J. J.

Time

CHAPTER 1

History of Time Measurement

What is time? Philosophers and scientists have puzzled over this question for centuries. Aristotle spoke of it as 'the number of motion' and Shakespeare makes Polonius avoid the issue by saying 'to expostulate . . . Why day is day, night, night, and time is time, Were nothing but to waste night, day, and time'. We too will avoid any philosophical discussion on the nature of time, and concentrate rather on the methods which have been and are being used to measure time intervals.

To measure the length of a room we could count the number of metre sticks which would fit, end to end, into it. To find the mass of a book we could count the number of 1 g masses ('weights') which would balance it. To find how long it takes for a train to travel from Aberdeen to London we could count the number of revolutions made by the minute hand of a watch during the journey. Measuring length, mass and time are really *counting* processes.

The metre unit of length and the kilogram unit of mass have been defined in terms of chunks of metal kept in France. A unit of time is not so easily defined. It is first necessary to find something which can be used as a standard time interval. *What properties must this standard possess?* (1) Each of us has a built-in time standard, which Galileo used in his first attempts to investigate the pendulum. *What is it?* (2) *What are its defects?* (3)

Clocks in the Sky

Thousands of years ago man knew that the 'heavenly spheres' moved with amazing regularity. It is not surprising then that calendars and clocks were based on such movements. The following descriptions of the solar day and sidereal day assume that the Earth rotates on its axis. Evidence for such a rotation was demonstrated in 1851 by the French physicist Foucault. He constructed a long pendulum, using 67 metres of wire and a lead ball of mass 28 kilograms. You can see a Foucault pendulum in the Royal Scottish Museum in Edinburgh. The following experiment will help you to understand its operation.

Experiment 1.1. Construct a long pendulum using strong thread and a small heavy object as the bob. Start the pendulum swinging, and very slowly twist the point of suspension. Does this alter the direction in which the pendulum swings?

The direction in which a Foucault pendulum swings is seen to rotate very gradually with respect to the Earth. But the direction

1

in which the pendulum swings relative to the fixed stars is always the same and so we conclude that the apparent rotation must be due to the spin of the Earth.

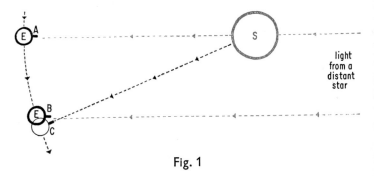

Fig. 1

The Earth spins on its axis once a day and rotates round the sun once a year. To obtain rather more precise definitions of 'day' and 'year' imagine that you have set up a telescope and fixed it so that it is focussed on a particular star (A in Fig. 1). When the Earth has rotated so that the same star is again seen in your telescope *a sidereal day* has elapsed and the Earth has moved to position B. If the telescope had been pointing to the sun at position A it would not be pointing to it in position B because of the Earth's motion round the sun. The Earth would have to continue spinning on its axis until it reached position C before the sun could be seen again in the telescope. The time taken for the Earth to move from position A to position C—a little over one complete revolution—is called a *solar day*. The solar day is about four minutes longer than the sidereal day. Astronomers use the sidereal day, but for most other purposes the average value of the solar day throughout the year is used. It is called the *mean solar day*.

The international unit of time is the *second*. Until recently it was defined as a fraction of the tropical year, which is the time the Earth takes to circle the sun between one equinox and the next corresponding equinox. The second was 1/31,556,925·9747 of the tropical year A.D. 1900.

Even this accuracy, of about 1 part in a billion, was not good enough for many physicists, astronomers and space technologists. In 1964 the International Bureau of Weights and Measures approved a new standard based on a natural frequency of the caesium atom. The new standard is about one hundred times more accurate and it is expected that even this accuracy will be increased considerably during the next few years.

The caesium clock shows that there are annual fluctuations in the Earth's rotation of the order of ±30 milliseconds.

Sundials

Shadow sticks have been used for thousands of years to indicate the time of day. It is thought that Cleopatra's Needle, erected 3,500 years ago in Egypt, may have been used as a sundial. If you push a stick vertically into the ground the direction of the shadow it casts will depend, to some extent, on the height of the sun. You can demonstrate this effect with a globe.

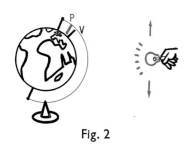

Fig. 2

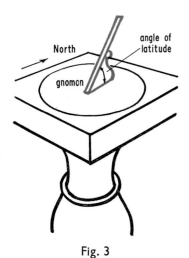

North

gnomon

angle of latitude

Fig. 3

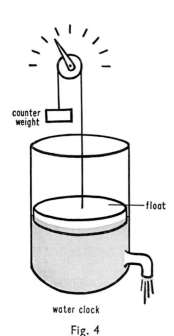

counter weight

float

water clock

Fig. 4

Demonstration 1.2. Use a piece of plasticine to fix a pin perpendicular to the surface of the globe of the world as shown in black (V) in Fig. 2. Illuminate the globe with a small source of light held some distance away and note the direction of the shadow. With the lamp fixed in one position rotate the globe and note how the direction of the shadow alters. Now vary the height of the lamp and see how the direction of the shadow alters with the globe stationary. Rotate the globe to various other positions and repeat the above.

Is there any position in which the direction of the shadow does not depend on the height of the lamp? Is there any time of day when the direction of the shadow of a vertical stick does not depend on the height of the sun?

Now fix the pin so that it is parallel to the Earth's axis (position P shown in red). In this position the angle between the pin and the Earth is equal to the latitude of the place where the pin is situated. Repeat the experiment with the pin in this new position. How does the height of the lamp (Sun) affect the direction of the shadow now?

The gnomon of a sundial should be set parallel to the Earth's axis as shown in Fig. 3. The time indicated on the dial is thus independent of the height of the sun, that is, of the time of the year. As the length of the solar day varies slightly throughout the year, however, the time registered differs from clock time which is mean solar time. *Can you think of another disadvantage of a sundial?* (4)

Clocks on the Earth

(a) Water Clocks

One of the earliest types of clocks which could be used at any time of the day or night was the water clock. In its simplest form this consisted of a bowl filled with water which escaped slowly from a tiny hole in the bottom. The amount of water left gave an indication of the time which had elapsed. A more sophisticated form used a float which operated a pointer (Fig. 4). Galileo used a water clock to investigate the acceleration of a ball rolling down an inclined plane.

Project 1.3. Construct a water clock from a burette, and use a stop watch to see if the water clock is accurate. Remembering the factors which govern the rate of flow of a fluid in a tube, can you explain the results?

(b) Sand Glasses

During the Middle Ages sand glasses were widely used to measure periods of time (Fig. 5). Today small sand glasses are still used as egg timers. Similar devices indicating a three minute period are sold for use with STD phone calls.

Project 1.4. Use a filter funnel and some fine dry sand to construct a simple sand glass.

Fig. 5

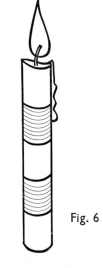

Fig. 6

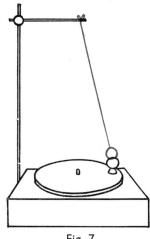

Fig. 7

(c) Oil Lamps and Candles

Calibrated candles and oil lamps fed from calibrated flasks were also used to measure time (Fig. 6).

(d) The Pendulum

The motion of a pendulum bob has been described as 'circular motion looked at sideways'. In the following experiment you should investigate the properties of a simple pendulum.

Experiment 1.5. Suspend a metal ball on a long thread and see how changing (1) the length (2) the mass and (3) the amplitude of the swing affects the *period*, that is, the time for a complete to and fro swing.

Demonstration 1.6. Fix a table tennis ball to a gramophone turntable and set up a pendulum so that the bob is just above it (Fig. 7). Use a 12 v car bulb to project shadows of the two spheres. Start the gramophone motor and the pendulum and adjust the length of the pendulum until both shadows are in step. Do they stay in step as the amplitude of the pendulum decreases? What does this suggest?

(e) Mechanical Clocks

Mechanical clocks, driven by falling 'weights,' were built about the 14th century, but they were never very accurate. It was not until the 17th century that Galileo's pendulum was used to control their rate of working. *What is the special feature of a pendulum which makes it well-suited to controlling a clock?* (5) *Describe how you would test your answer by experiment.* (6)

In the system illustrated in Fig. 8 the escape wheel is connected to the clock mechanism and is thus driven by a weight or by a spring. As the pendulum swings it rocks the escapement, thus allowing the escape wheel to turn by one tooth at the end of each swing. At the same time the pendulum receives a tiny kick from the escape wheel. The pendulum is thus kept swinging as long as the escape wheel is being driven

In watches and small clocks the suspended pendulum is replaced by a balance wheel and hairspring (torsional pendulum), which oscillate to and fro rather like the spring and flywheel illustrated in Book 1, Fig. 199.

Project 1.7. Examine the mechanisms of a pendulum clock and a watch—after asking the owner's permission!

Errors

You have, no doubt, been introduced to 'experimental error' as the demon responsible for preventing school experiments giving the expected results. This is not just an excuse. Scientists spend a great deal of time and energy trying to find the causes, and ways of reducing, such errors.

If you were asked to measure the length of a metal block you might give the answer '10 centimetres'. If you were very accurate you might measure it as 10·1 centimetres. Only a scientist using accurate research equipment could give an answer correct to a thousandth of a centimetre, that is, accurate to one part in 10,000,

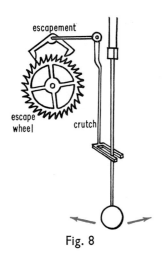

escapement

escape wheel

crutch

Fig. 8

or 1 in 10^4. If the error were 1 in 10,000, that is 0·01 in 100, it would be referred to as an error of 0·01 per cent.

Although we would not normally expect this kind of accuracy in measuring length or mass, a wrist watch may lose or gain no more than 10 seconds a day, that is

$$10 \text{ parts in } 60 \times 60 \times 24$$

$$\frac{10}{60 \times 60 \times 24} = \frac{1}{8640}$$

$$= \frac{1}{10000} \text{ (approximately)}$$

$$= 0\cdot01 \text{ per cent approximately}$$

A chronometer about the size of a pocket watch was built in 1759 for which an accuracy of $4\frac{1}{2}$ seconds in 10 weeks was claimed. Find the approximate percentage error. (7)

(f) Electric Clocks

Clocks which operate from A.C. mains are driven by synchronous motors. The speed of such motors is controlled by the frequency of the supply. *What is this frequency in Britain?* (8) The following demonstration illustrates the principle of the synchronous motor.

tinplate disc

coil

soft iron core

Fig. 9

Demonstration 1.8. A simple motor may be constructed from a disc of tin plate. It should be free to rotate near an electro-magnet as shown in Fig. 9. Connect the electro-magnet to the output terminals of a variable transformer₁ and gradually increase the voltage applied while spinning the disc.

Once the motor is running at a constant speed illuminate it with a mains operated neon lamp. Can you explain the result produced?

(g) Quartz Crystal Clocks

You have already heard of the piezo-electric effect (Book 2, page 117). Because of this effect the frequency of an electronic oscillator can be controlled by a quartz crystal kept at a constant temperature. Some VHF radio receivers are crystal controlled.

In 1935 quartz crystal clocks were developed by the National Physical Laboratory. They were capable of an accuracy of 1 part in 10^8, that is, to within a second in three years.

(h) Atomic Clocks

We might be forgiven for thinking that it would be impossible to improve on an accuracy of a second in three years, yet atomic clocks have now been developed with an accuracy better than one second in a century! What is even more amazing is the fact that this kind of accuracy is available in every home. The BBC 'pips' are controlled by an atomic clock.

The international standard of time is now checked by the caesium atomic clock.

Time Signals

Over a hundred years ago hourly signals were sent out by telegraph from the Royal Greenwich Observatory. They were used to operate *time balls*. These balls were fixed to masts on top of tall buildings and released at certain times. One was situated in Greenwich so that ships could check their chronometers, and another in the Strand for the benefit of Londoners. One such ball is still released every day at 1 p.m. from a mast on the Nelson Column in Edinburgh. At the same time the famous 'one-o'clock gun' is fired from the Castle for the benefit of those who cannot see the Nelson Column.

In 1924 the BBC first radiated regular time signals. They were controlled by a pendulum clock until 1946, when crystal clocks were introduced. Atomic clocks are now used.

For scientific purposes the National Physical Laboratory broadcasts time signals, 24 hours a day, from Rugby. They are broadcast on 2·5 mc/s and 5 mc/s and the station is identified by the letters MSF in morse code. Unfortunately these signals are very weak and a communication receiver is usually necessary to receive them. Most of the time this station broadcasts one-second 'ticks'. If you *can* receive them you might like to set up a simple pendulum to keep in step with them. As those ticks are accurate to about one second per century you can also use them to check your watch!

Measuring Short Time Intervals

When studying physical processes it is often necessary to measure very short intervals of time. We will consider various methods of doing this and discuss their advantages and disadvantages. We will look for accuracy, simplicity and any effects the timing mechanism may have on the system being timed.

Fig. 10

(a) Stop Watch

A stop watch is perhaps the most straightforward device for measuring short time intervals. Although the watch itself may be very accurate it is not suitable for measuring time intervals of the order of one second. Can you discover why this is from the following experiments?

Experiment 1.9. Use a stop watch to measure the time taken for a ball to fall to the floor from a height of about 6 feet. Compare your results with those obtained (a) by other people, (b) by yourself when you repeat the experiment several times.

Experiment 1.10. Ask a group of pupils to join hands in a circle, leaving a gap for you (Fig. 10). Now start a stop watch and at the same instant tap the shoulder of the person on your left. He should then grasp his neighbour's hand very firmly. This grasping process is repeated round the circle, and the last pupil can tap your shoulder when he receives the message. Stop the watch then and calculate the average time taken by each pupil to react. Repeat this experiment with all eyes closed!

Experiment 1.11. For this experiment a stop watch in which the hand moves round once every six seconds is suitable. Stick a piece of paper over the face so that the hand is visible for exactly two seconds during each revolution (Fig. 11).

Now use another stop watch—the most accurate one you can find—to measure the time during which the hand is visible. Start the second watch as soon as you see the hand and stop the watch when the hand disappears. Try this several times and compare the results.

Fig. 11

When you see something happening you do not react to it immediately. There is a time lag, usually of a fraction of a second, which varies from person to person. This is called a *reaction time*. If, for example, you did not press the stop watch button in Experiment 1.11 until 0·3 seconds after the hand appeared your reaction time would be 0·3 seconds. Of course if you took 0·3 seconds to press the button after the hand had disappeared you would measure the time interval correctly. Human reaction times are however rarely as consistent as this, particularly when the conditions are different at the beginning and the end of the period being measured. In this experiment you have no warning of the hand's appearance but you can see when it is about to disappear. This will affect your reaction time.

Is there any point in having a manually operated stop watch calibrated to read thousandths of a second? Explain your answer. (9)

(b) Electric Stop Clock

Electric stop clocks are normally controlled by the mains frequency (50 c/s) and are capable of reading accurately to a hundredth of a second or less. They may be switched directly by making or breaking mechanical contacts, or indirectly by interrupting a beam of light. Such clocks are useful for timing a body falling freely.

Fig. 12

Fig. 13

Fig. 14

Project 1.12. Can you devise an experiment using an electric stop clock$_2$, such as the one illustrated in Fig. 12, to find your reaction time? One method uses a morse key to start the clock and another to stop it. When you see and hear the first key being closed you press the second key which stops the clock.

(c) Counter

A scaler is normally used, with a Geiger-Muller tube, to count the number of atomic particles striking the end of the tube. It may however be used to count other things. Some counters are fitted with oscillators which produce 1000 pulses a second. By using the counter to count these pulses we turn it into a clock. If it is switched on for one second the counter will read 1000, after running for three seconds it will read 3000 and so on. Thus we can measure time intervals to one thousandth of a second, provided our switching arrangements are very good!

(d) Hand Stroboscope

A good estimate of the frequency of a vibrating or rotating object can be obtained with a very simple piece of apparatus. It consists of a hardboard disc with a number of slits in it$_3$. By looking through the disc as it is rotated the motion can be 'stopped'.

Experiment 1.13.

(i) Using opaque adhesive tape cover all but one of the slits on a hand stroboscope, and use it to time a rotating gramophone turntable. To do this place on the turntable a cardboard disc with a white radial line marked on it, (Fig. 13), and illuminate it with a powerful lamp (e.g. a photoflood bulb). View the turntable through the strobe disc and vary the speed of the strobe disc until the turntable appears stationary. Can you make it appear stationary at a higher or at a lower strobe speed? Find the *highest* strobe speed at which the motion is 'stopped' without double viewing. When the disc is rotating at this speed ask your partner to find its speed by timing (say) 20 revolutions of the strobe disc with a stop watch. How is this strobe speed related to the turntable speed? Calculate the number of revolutions of the turntable. Why should your partner not time only one revolution?

Remove the tape from the stroboscope slit opposite the open one, and repeat this experiment. If the turntable appears stationary with different strobe speeds, which is the correct one? Why?

(ii) Clamp a hacksaw blade to a bench and stick a lump of plasticine on the end (Fig. 14). Using a stroboscope disc with 2 open slits try to find the frequency of the vibrating blade. What is the relationship between the number of revolutions per second of the strobe disc and the frequency of the blade?

Now reduce the size of the plasticine lump. How does this affect the vibration frequency? Using 4 or 6 open slits, equally spaced, find the vibration frequency.

(iii) Use the hand stroboscope with 6 or 12 equally spaced open slits to find the frequency of the clapper of an electric bell or a ticker-tape timer (Fig. 15).

Fig. 15

Fig. 16 (a)

Fig.16 (b)

In a ticker-tape timer$_{3,4}$ the clapper strikes a disc of carbon paper under which paper tape is pulled. Dots are therefore produced on the paper at the frequency of the clapper. You can find this frequency by pulling the tape through a timer for (say) five seconds and counting the number of dots produced. In this way you can calibrate the timer, which may then be used to measure intervals of time.

Problems

10. *If a length of tape is pulled through a timer vibrating at 30 c/s and 75 dots are marked on the tape, for how long has the tape been moving?*

11. *If a 12-slit strobe disc rotating at 3 revolutions per second 'stops' a vibrator, what is the frequency of the vibrator? You may assume this is the highest strobe speed which does not give double viewing.*

Project 1.14. Having found the frequency of a ticker-tape timer devise an experiment to find how long a block of wood takes to fall 1 metre vertically. State any sources of inaccuracy in your experiment.

(e) Stroboscope Lamp

There are various flashing lamps (stroboscopes) on the market. They normally consist of a gas-filled tube (e.g. neon or xenon) which flashes off and on at a frequency which can be altered by the operator. Strobe lamps$_{5,19}$ may be used to find the speed at which something is turning, for example, a lathe.

Explain why a lathe turning in one direction can appear to be turning in the opposite direction when illuminated by a strobe lamp. (12) *Why do the wheels of a car, seen on a cinema screen, often appear to be turning the wrong way?* (13) *Can you explain the operation of the discs used when adjusting the speed of gramophone turntables?* (14) *Can they be used in daylight? Explain your answer.* (15)

Experiment 1.15.

(a) Paint a white spot on the shaft of an electric motor or on motor-driven disc₃ and illuminate it with a stroboscope lamp. Switch on the motor, and when it has reached a steady speed adjust the strobe frequency until the shaft appears to stand still.

What happens when the strobe frequency is (i) halved and (ii) doubled? Look for the *highest* strobe frequency at which the shaft appears stationary without giving a 'double image' of the white spot. This is the frequency of rotation of the shaft.

(b) Find the frequency of an electric bell or timer using the calibrations on the strobe lamp. Compare your results with those obtained with the hand strobe.

(f) Stroboscopic Photography

A strobe lamp may be used to photograph a moving object. The camera shutter is left open and a series of images then appear on the photographic plate. Fig. 17 shows a photograph produced

Fig. 17

Fig. 18

in this way. As there were 10 flashes per second the time interval between each image is $\frac{1}{10}$ of a second. The half-metre stick in the picture enables us to calculate how far the car travelled in $\frac{1}{10}$th of a second.

Instead of keeping the camera shutter open and switching the light off and on, you can take this kind of photograph by keeping the car illuminated all the time and opening and closing the camera shutter 10 times a second. The simplest way of doing this is to place a disc with (say) 2 slits in it in front of the camera and arrange that the disc₃ is rotated 5 times a second by a synchronous motor (Fig. 18). As before, 10 photographs are taken each second, so that the time interval between each is $\frac{1}{10}$th of a second. Opaque adhesive tape can be used to cover unwanted slits.

(g) Vibrators

In the experiment with the hacksaw blade (Experiment 1.13) you discovered that such a metal strip vibrates at a natural frequency. This frequency is altered, however, if a piece of plasticine or a crocodile clip is attached to the end of the strip. *Does the plasticine reduce or increase the frequency?* (16) *How would you expect the note of a tuning fork to be altered if pieces of plasticine were stuck on the ends of the prongs? Try this and see if your prediction was correct.* (17)

A tuning fork is a good example of a simple vibrator whose frequency is constant. By means of a suitable circuit, not unlike that of an electric bell, tuning forks can be made to vibrate continuously. The frequency of radio transmitters used to be controlled by electrically operated tuning forks. Some modern wrist watches use tiny electrically-maintained tuning forks. An accuracy of about 2 seconds per day is claimed for them. A ticker-tape timer is rather like an electrically maintained tuning fork. The armature of the timer vibrates at a natural frequency and this is kept going electrically.

There are many ways of using vibrators to measure short time intervals. These include attaching inked brushes to pendulums or vibrating metal strips. The ticker-tape timer is, however, the simplest device for our present purposes.

Problem 18. A timer is 'stopped' without double viewing at a top speed of 4 revs per second using a 6-slit strobe disc. Find the frequency of the vibrator. If someone pulls paper tape through the timer and his partner switches the timer on for 3 seconds how many dots should be marked on the paper? How could this method be used to measure a short period of time? What are the snags?

Measuring Long Time Intervals

By taking a movie film at (say) one frame per day and projecting it at 24 frames per second a process which takes months to complete can be seen in a few seconds. The growth of plants, for example, can be studied by such *time-lapse* photography.

In his science fiction tale 'Before the Dawn' Professor Bell describes a fantastic kind of television set on which events which occurred millions of years ago may be seen today. By the twist of a knob any part of ancient history may be re-enacted. Although such a device must remain fictional the discovery of radioactivity has enabled modern geologists to estimate the age of rocks and even the Earth itself. Radioactive elements slowly change (disintegrate) with time, and by measuring the fraction which is unchanged the age of the element may be calculated. By this method it has been estimated that some of the Earth's rocks are about four and a half thousand million years old. Contrast this with the time taken for light to pass through a window—a hundred thousand millionth of a second!

Visual Aids

Charts; Time$_{24}$ C.627.
Filmstrips: The Story of Time$_{24}$ 6007.
Time and Direction$_{24}$ 5092.
16 mm Films: How to Measure Time$_{23}$ 21.7482.

Distance and Displacement

CHAPTER 2

How Far?

If you travel 142 miles from Edinburgh to Aberdeen and then 142 miles from Aberdeen to Glasgow (a) *how far have you gone and* (b) *how far are you from Edinburgh?* (1)

These questions are quite different. The first asks for the total distance covered during your northward trip and your southward trip. It asks for the *distance* travelled. The second asks for the *shortest* distance between Edinburgh and Glasgow. *Measure this distance on a map and use the given scale to calculate the actual distance.* (2)

The distance, 'as the crow flies', from the starting point to the finishing point is called the *displacement*. *Under what conditions would the distance gone and the displacement be numerically equal?* (3)

If on a round trip you cycle 40 miles and then arrive back home (a) *what distance have you travelled and* (b) *what is your final displacement?* (4)

Vectors

A cricketer runs 20 yards from A to B (Fig. 19) and then 18 yards on his return run before being run out. What was his displacement from A when the bails were knocked off? (5) If he had run 2 yards past A

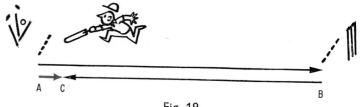

Fig. 19

his displacement from A would still have been 2 yards yet he would be in a very different position. If displacement has to describe the length AC shown in Fig. 19 we will need to know not only that it is 2 yards (*magnitude*) but also that it is measured along the line AB from A (*direction*).

If the cricket pitch lies east–west, we could describe the final displacement as 2 yards east from A.

It is often convenient to represent quantities such as displacement by a line and arrow head. The magnitude of the displacement is represented by the length of the line and the direction of the displacement is shown by the arrow.

The arrows may be anywhere on the line and may have a variety of forms. In this book we will normally use an arrow as shown in Fig. 20. Lines of this kind are called *vectors*. The quantities represented by vectors are called *vector quantities*.

Fig. 20

Displacement is a vector quantity, that is, it is fully described only when both its magnitude and direction are indicated. When a quantity can be described fully by a number (magnitude) and the appropriate units, it is called a scalar quantity. Distance is a scalar quantity.

State whether the following are vector quantities or scalar quantities: force, mass, length, temperature, weight, volume, density. (6)

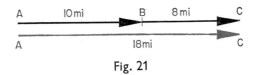

Fig. 21

If a car travels 10 miles in a straight line and then a further 8 miles in the same direction its *resultant displacement* will be 18 miles (Fig. 21). If $\overrightarrow{AB}$ represents a displacement of 10 miles and $\overrightarrow{BC}$ a displacement of 8 miles the resultant is represented by $\overrightarrow{AC}$. We will always show the resultant in red.

$$\overrightarrow{AB} + \overrightarrow{BC} = \overrightarrow{AC}$$

If two vectors are joined, tip to tail, in a straight line their resultant is represented by a line from the tail of the first to the tip of the second.

Resultant Displacement

Let us now return to our cricketer and represent his displacements by vectors. Had he stopped at B (Fig. 19) his displacement would have been represented by $\overrightarrow{AB}$. $\overrightarrow{BC}$ represents a displacement from B in the opposite direction. $\overrightarrow{AC}$ represents the *resultant displacement* from his starting point A. Note that although the *vectors* $\overrightarrow{AB} + \overrightarrow{BC}$ add up to the vector $\overrightarrow{AC}$ the *distances* AB + BC do not add up to the distance AC.

Vector Addition

To add two displacements which are not in a straight line we use a scale drawing. If a snail crawls eastwards for 3 metres and then northwards for 4 metres, how far is it from the start? Its final displacement can be found from Fig. 22. Notice that the two vectors which we are adding (that is $\overrightarrow{SE}$ and $\overrightarrow{EN}$) follow each other as shown.

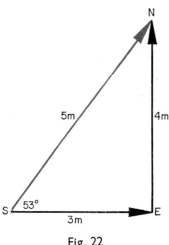

Fig. 22

From Pythagoras' theorem, or by measuring a scale drawing, we see that the magnitude of the resultant displacement is 5 metres. Its direction is 53° north of east.

VECTOR ADDITION

$$\overrightarrow{SE} + \overrightarrow{EN} = \overrightarrow{SN}$$
$$\overrightarrow{3} + \overrightarrow{4} = \overrightarrow{5}$$

SCALAR ADDITION

$$3 + 4 = 7$$

We have considered two special cases where vectors making angles of 90° and 180° with each other were added together. The scale drawing (geometrical) method can, however, be used to find the resultant of two vectors making any angle with one another.

Fig. 23 is a vector diagram representing a displacement of 6 miles eastwards from A, followed by a displacement from B of 5 miles 20° north of west. AC then gives the resultant displacement.

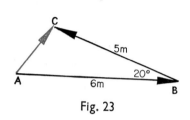

Fig. 23

$$\overrightarrow{AB} + \overrightarrow{BC} = \overrightarrow{AC}$$

This type of vector addition is applicable to all vector quantities and the resultant AC is referred to as the *vector sum.*

Problems

7. *A cyclist travels northwards for 2 miles and then turns right through 45°. He continues in this direction for 3 miles. Use a large scale drawing to find his resultant displacement. Remember to put arrows on the lines you draw. Otherwise they are not vectors!*

8. *A car travels south for 5 miles and then 20° east of south for 5 miles. Find, by scale drawing, the resultant displacement.*

Simultaneous Displacements

In our previous examples, displacements occurred one after the other. It is possible, however, for a body to be displaced in two directions at once. A man walking across a railway carriage in motion is an example of this.

Demonstration 2.1. A horizontal perspex tube containing a ball can be pushed up a vertical board (Fig. 24). The ball therefore moves vertically and its displacement is represented by the vertical vector. If a thread is attached to the ball it can be pulled horizontally and its displacement represented by the horizontal vector. If either end of the thread is now attached to the board, as shown, the ball will move along the tube when the tube is moved vertically. The actual path of the ball relative to the board is clearly seen to be the *resultant.*

Problem 9. A river is 100 metres wide and flows from north to south. In the time taken to cross the river a man finds that his boat has drifted 75 metres downstream. Find by scale drawing, the man's resultant displacement on reaching the other side. Remember that you must state both distance and direction to specify displacement.

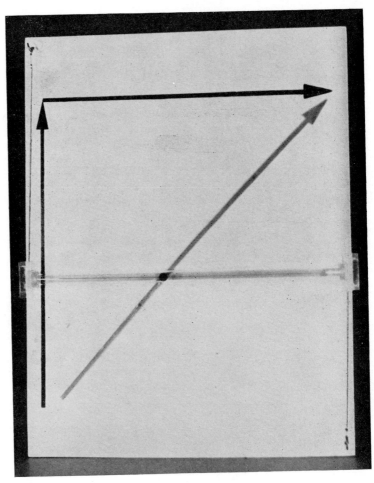

Fig. 24

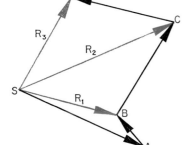

Fig. 25

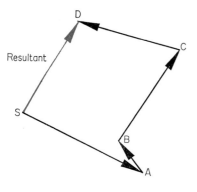

Fig. 26

Optional Extras

In Fig. 25 $\overrightarrow{SB}$ (or $\overrightarrow{R_1}$ for short) is the resultant of $\overrightarrow{SA} + \overrightarrow{AB}$. As far as displacement is concerned $\overrightarrow{R_1}$ is equivalent to $\overrightarrow{SA} + \overrightarrow{AB}$ and can therefore replace them. If now we add $\overrightarrow{R_1}$ and $\overrightarrow{BC}$ together the resultant will be $\overrightarrow{R_2}$. $\overrightarrow{R_2}$ is therefore the resultant of $\overrightarrow{SA} + \overrightarrow{AB} + \overrightarrow{BC}$. Similarly $\overrightarrow{R_3}$ is the resultant of $\overrightarrow{R_2} + \overrightarrow{CD}$ and therefore represents the resultant of $\overrightarrow{SA} + \overrightarrow{AB} + \overrightarrow{BC} + \overrightarrow{CD}$.

Provided a series of vectors are joined tail to tip we can find the resultant of all the vectors by joining the first and the last points (Fig. 26).

Problems

10. *A man walks 1 mile east, 2 miles north, 3 miles south-west and half a mile south-east. Find his resultant displacement from the starting point.*

11. An aeroplane flies south for 20 miles, south-south-west for 5 miles, north-west for 10 miles, then north-east for 30 miles. Find its resultant displacement.

Frames of Reference

Demonstration 2.2. Place a wooden board or sheet of hardboard on a flat bench or table. Place a revving flywheel-driven car on the board and push the board across the table at right angles to the car's motion (Fig. 27). The board moves over the table surface as the car moves along the board.

Fig. 27

The movement of the car can be considered as two separate motions. In the first place the board moves relative to the table. This is represented by the vector $\overrightarrow{TB}$ in Fig. 28. Secondly the car moves relative to the board. $\overrightarrow{BC}$ represents this movement.

Imagine that the car is driven by a dwarf who has spent all his life on this board. He knows no other 'world', and for him the board is not moving. For him the car would move in a straight line across the board. The board is his *'frame of reference'*. On such a frame of reference the car's displacement would be represented by $\overrightarrow{BC}$. In dealing with some vector quantities, such as displacement, it is convenient to letter the tail and the tip of the vector as shown in Fig. 29.

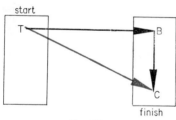

Fig. 28

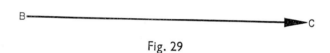

Fig. 29

This means that the car (C) has been displaced by this amount *relative to the board* (B). We will use this method later with velocities.

Like the dwarf we have no direct awareness of the motion of our world, and the Earth's surface is our normal frame of reference. For most practical purposes we assume that the Earth is stationary and we measure distances from a point on its surface. When we say that a train is travelling at 80 mi/h we ignore the Earth's 70,000 mi/h flight round the sun and refer only to the train's speed relative to the Earth.

In our experiment with the toy car the table, as part of the Earth's surface, is our frame of reference, so that we measure the final displacement ($\overrightarrow{TC}$) of the car from the starting point on the table. Notice that the frame of reference may be identified by the point to which the tails of the two vectors are attached. Notice also that the vector $\overrightarrow{TC}$ does not necessarily indicate the *path* of the car. It merely indicates the distance between the starting and finishing points and the direction in which the car finishes relative to the point where it started. *Under what conditions would the car move in a straight line between T and C?* (12)

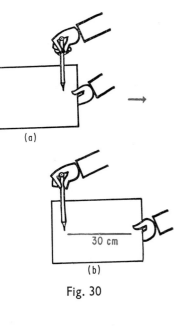

(a)

30 cm

(b)

Fig. 30

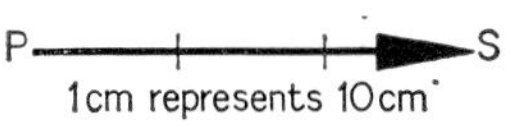

Imagine that a pencil is held so that it touches a sheet of paper (Fig. 30a). If the paper is then pulled in the direction of the arrow, a line will be drawn as shown in Fig. 30b. If this line is 30 cm long the displacement could be represented by the vector (say) 3 cm long. As the pencil is stationary relative to the Earth we would take the pencil (P) as our frame of reference. The displacement of the sheet (S) would then be represented by the vector shown in Fig. 31.

We might, however, take the sheet of paper as our frame of reference, and in this case the pencil would be seen to move relative to the paper. A vector representing this displacement is shown in Fig. 32.

Notice that in each case the tail of the arrow indicates the frame of reference.

Problem 13. A teacher holds a piece of chalk against a roller blackboard and moves the chalk 50 cm horizontally. During this time someone pulls the board down 30 cm. Draw a vector diagram showing.

the displacement of the board (B) relative to the Earth (E),
the displacement of the chalk (C) relative to the Earth (E) and
the displacement of the chalk (C) relative to the board (B).

Which is the resultant displacement, using the Earth as your frame of reference?
Now draw a vector diagram using the blackboard as your frame of reference. The vectors should represent the movement of

the chalk (C) relative to the board (B)
the Earth (E) relative to the board (B)
and the chalk (C) relative to the Earth (E)

What is the resultant displacement now?

P——————————►S
1cm represents 10cm

Fig. 31

P◄——————————S
1cm represents 10cm

Fig. 32

Visual Aids

Charts: Vectors$_{24}$ C.785.

Speed and Velocity

CHAPTER 3

Speed

In order to travel at 3,600 mi/h a rocket need not travel for one hour. If it travelled for only one minute and covered 60 miles it would be said to have a speed of 3,600 mi/h. If it travelled for only one second and went 1 mile it would still have a speed of 3,600 mi/h during that second. What then is the smallest time interval during which a rocket can be said to have a certain speed? You might say that the interval could be 'as small as you like'. If, however, the time interval were *zero* the distance gone would also be *zero*, from which it is not easy to calculate a speed! To help us out of this dilemma we can use the symbol Δ (pronounced 'delta'—Greek for 'a wee bit'!!). A small time interval is then written as Δt which means that it can be 'as small as you like' *provided it is not quite zero*. The corresponding distance gone in that small time interval is then labelled Δd.

$$\text{rocket speed} = \frac{3,600 \text{ miles}}{1 \text{ hour}} = 3,600 \text{ mi/h}$$

$$\text{or } \frac{60 \text{ miles}}{1/60 \text{ hour}} = 60 \times 60 = 3,600 \text{ mi/h}$$

$$\text{or } \frac{1 \text{ mile}}{1/3,600 \text{ hour}} = \frac{1}{1} \times 3,600 = 3,600 \text{ mi/h}$$

$$speed = \frac{\Delta s}{\Delta t} \qquad \text{or } \frac{\Delta d}{\Delta t} \text{ where } \Delta d \text{ is the distance gone in a very small interval of time } \Delta t$$

Using SI units we have:

$$v = \frac{s}{t}$$

$$\text{speed } (v) = \frac{\text{distance gone } (d) \quad \text{metres}}{\text{time } (t) \quad \text{seconds}}$$

metres/second

Average Speed

If you were travelling along a motorway at a uniform speed, with the speedometer reading a steady 80 mi/h, it is true that in 1 hour you would travel 80 miles and you could say that your speed was 80 mi/h. On most British roads, however, your speed would be altering all the time and you might find that you have travelled only 40 miles in one hour. In such a case we could speak of an *average speed* of 40 mi/h, although at various times during that hour your speedometer may have read 80 mi/h, 60 mi/h, 20 mi/h,

18

10 mi/h and zero. If you have travelled at a *constant speed* of 40 mi/h for one hour you would have covered the same distance.

$$\text{average speed} = \frac{\text{total distance travelled}}{\text{total time taken}}$$

Experiment 3.1. Measure out (say) 30 metres in a corridor and use a stopwatch to time your partner (i) walking, (ii) running and (iii) moving at different speeds along the corridor. Calculate his average speed in each case and express it in metres per second.

Experiment 3.2.

(*a*) Ask your partner to walk a few steps at different speeds while pulling a length of ticker-tape through a timer$_{3,4}$ (Fig. 33). Find the timer frequency and calculate your partner's average speed from the tape.

(*b*) Now cut the ticker tape into lengths of (say) 10 spaces. Each length will represent the distance your partner has gone in 10 short time intervals (10 ticks), that is, it represents his speed. If the timer vibrates at 50 c/s each length of tape will represent the distance gone in one fifth of a second.

Now stick these lengths of tape, in order, on a sheet of graph paper (Fig. 34). You have now constructed a tape chart which is a kind of graph showing your partner's speed plotted against time.

How can you tell when your partner was (*a*) speeding up (*b*) going at a steady speed, and (*c*) slowing down?

Problems

1. *Describe the motion represented by each of the speed/time graphs in Fig. 35. Could Figs. (a) and (b) represent the same motion? Explain your answer.*

2. *A timer producing 50 dots per second is used to find the average speed of a trolley. The distance between the first and tenth dots is 20 cm. Was the speed of the trolley 1 m/s? Explain your answer.*

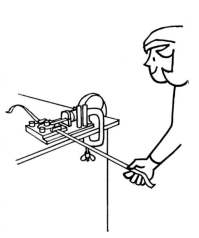

Fig. 33

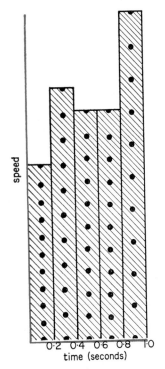

0·2 0·4 0·6 0·8 1·0
time (seconds)

Fig. 34

Velocity

Imagine you set out one morning from a hostel in the Cairngorms and walk through valleys and over hills and crags until in the late afternoon you welcome the sight of an old shooting-lodge resting in the valley by the side of a river. You have been on your feet for 7 hours and have covered 21 miles. Your average speed has been 3 mi/h. Having identified the hostel and the shooting-lodge on a map you discover that they are only 5 miles apart as the crow flies—or the mole burrows. Your displacement from the hostel is 5 miles. It is sometimes useful to know your speed in one direction, that is, the displacement per unit of time. This quantity is called the velocity.

$$v = \frac{s}{t}$$

$$\text{velocity } (v) = \frac{\text{displacement } (d)}{\text{time } (t)}$$

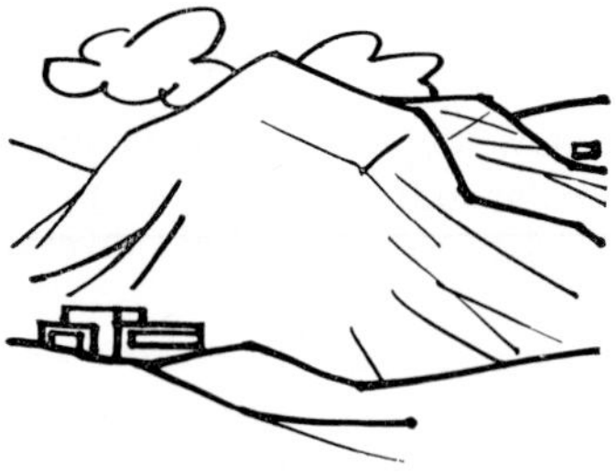

Fig. 36

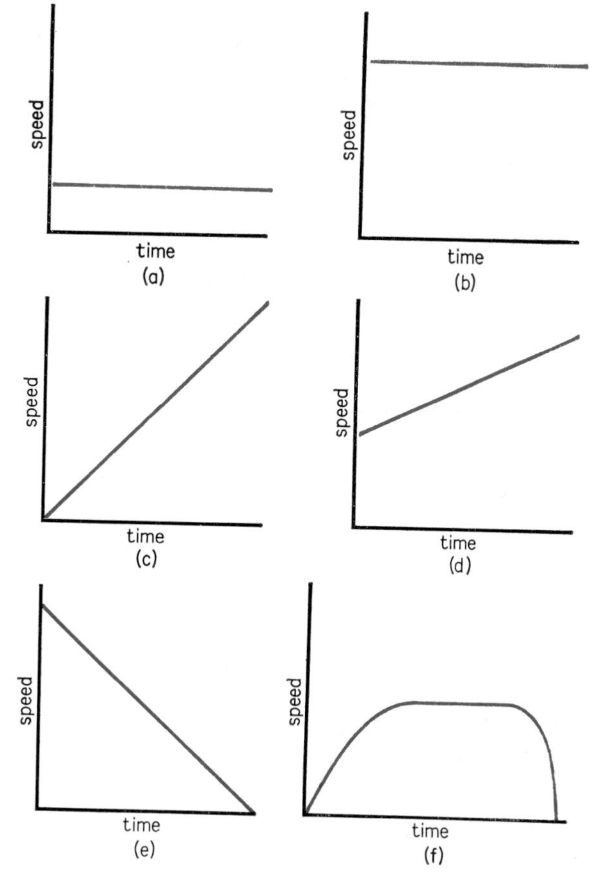

Fig. 35

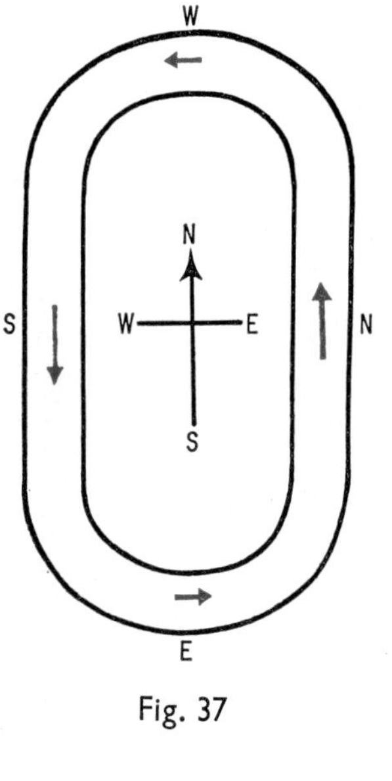

Fig. 37

Displacement is a *vector quantity*: velocity is also a *vector quantity*, and therefore its magnitude and direction should both be stated. Your average velocity from the hostel to the shooting-lodge might be stated as $\frac{5}{7}$ mi/h S.E. Note carefully that the direction should be stated as otherwise you are indicating a speed of $\frac{5}{7}$ mi/h, which is completely wrong as we have already calculated the average speed as 3 mi/h.

A speedway track is situated as shown in Fig. 37. If a rider is moving north (N) at 60 mi/h on the straight his speed is 60 mi/h and his velocity is 60 mi/h north. At the corner his speed is 40 mi/h so that at W his velocity is 40 mi/h west. His velocity north is now zero. At S he is travelling 60 mi/h south and his velocity west is zero. We could also say that at S his velocity was *minus* 60 mi/h north. *If his speed at E is 40 mi/h, what then is his velocity in each of the four compass directions?* (3)

Rectilinear Motion

In most of the problems with which we shall have to deal, motion will be in straight lines, so that speed and velocity will be numerically equal. In practice 'velocity' is often used to denote the magnitude of the velocity vector, that is, the speed. They may both be represented by v. Motion in a straight line is called *rectilinear motion*.

Speedometer

The simplest method of finding the speed of a body moving in a straight line is to read a speedometer fitted to it. This was suggested for the playground trolley illustrated in Book 1 (p. 100, Fig. 159). It is not possible, however, to fit speedometers to everything whose speed you want to measure. This is particularly true of atoms and molecules.

Project 3.3. You might like to try to build a simple speedometer for yourself using a dynamo and a meter to read the output voltage. Can you think of a way of using this to indicate (say) your speed as you walk across the room?

Stroboscopic Photographs

In the laboratory one of the most useful ways of finding the speed of a moving object is to photograph it stroboscopically.

Fig. 38 shows a photograph of a moving object to which a drinking straw has been attached. The pictures were taken every tenth of a second. *What kind of motion does this photograph show?* (4)

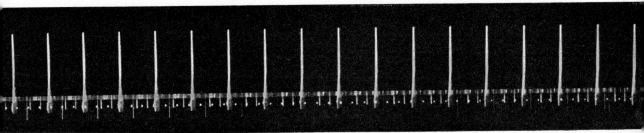

Fig. 38

Fig. 48 (page 26) also shows a strobe photograph. When is the speed of the white spot greatest in the direction of the arrow? (5) *When is it least?* (6) *What can you say about the speed of the centre of the disc, as indicated by the small white dot?* (7)

Ticker Tape

You have already used a ticker timer to find your speed. *How would you find out how many dots it produced every second?* (8)

Fig. 39 shows a piece of tape marked by a timer producing 50 dots per second. *Does this represent a uniform speed?* (9) *What is the average speed between A and D? Give your answers in cm/s*

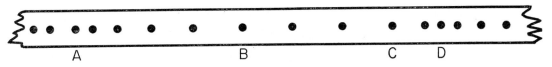

Fig. 39

and m/s. (10) *What are the greatest and the least speeds indicated?* (11) *Does the distance between two adjacent dots indicate an instantaneous or average speed?* (12) *What is happening to the speed between A and B?* (13) *How does the speed vary between B and C?* (14) *Does the speed indicated by the tape suggest that it might have been produced by a snail crawling, a boy walking, a car racing or an aeroplane in flight?* (15)

Graphs

You have constructed graphs using strips of ticker tape, each strip representing the distance gone in a given time. If, for example, the length of the tape is 5 cm and this was produced in 10 ticks (i.e. $\frac{1}{5}$ second), this represents a speed of 5 cm per $\frac{1}{5}$ second or 25 cm/s. Instead of sticking the strips on the graph paper you could measure the length of each strip and plot its length (as a measure of speed) directly on the graph paper.

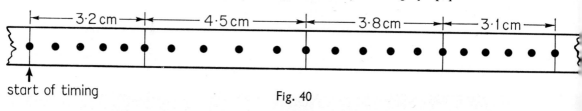

start of timing

Fig. 40

Let us imagine that the timer marks 5 dots per second. The length of 5 spaces will then represent the distance gone in one second. If this length is 3·2 cm the average speed during that second is 3·2 cm/s (Fig. 40). This can be represented on the graph by the line AB on Fig. 41. Notice that this is not necessarily the first

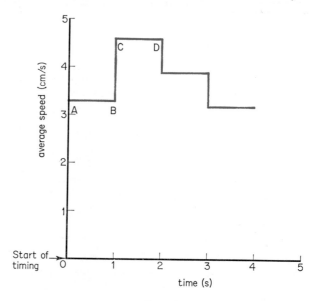

Fig. 41

second of the motion; it is the first second during which we *measure* it. During the next second the body moves 4·5 cm so that the average speed is 4·5 cm/s. This is represented by the line CD. By continuing in this way we can construct a graph of the speed plotted against time. It is very unlikely that the motion represented by this graph actually jumped in steps like this. But then we were dealing with the average speed over a second. If we had measured the average speed each fifth of a second, we might have obtained a graph such as that shown in Fig. 42. Similarly, had we been able

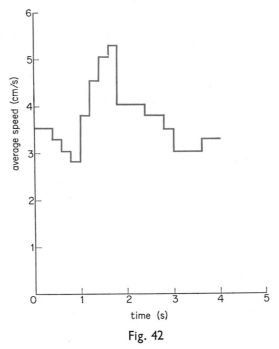

Fig. 42

to measure the speed every 50th of a second, it might have looked more like Fig. 43.

Strictly speaking it is the average speed we are finding, even when the time interval is 1/50th of a second, but in practice we drop the 'average' when referring to speed measured over small fractions of a second.

Area Under a Graph

If a body is moving at a constant speed of 4 m/s its motion could be represented by the graph PQRST shown in Fig. 44. Using the units indicated the areas could be calculated as follows.

$$\text{Area A} = 4 \text{ m/s} \times 1 \text{ s} = 4 \frac{m}{s} \times s = 4 \text{ m}$$

$$\text{Area B} = 4 \text{ m/s} \times 1 \text{ s} = 4 \frac{m}{s} \times s = 4 \text{ m}$$

$$\text{Area C} = 4 \text{ m/s} \times 1 \text{ s} = 4 \frac{m}{s} \times s = 4 \text{ m}$$

$$\text{Area D} = 4 \text{ m/s} \times 1 \text{ s} = 4 \frac{m}{s} \times s = 4 \text{ m}$$

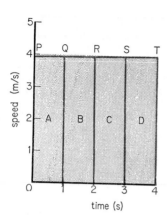

Fig. 44

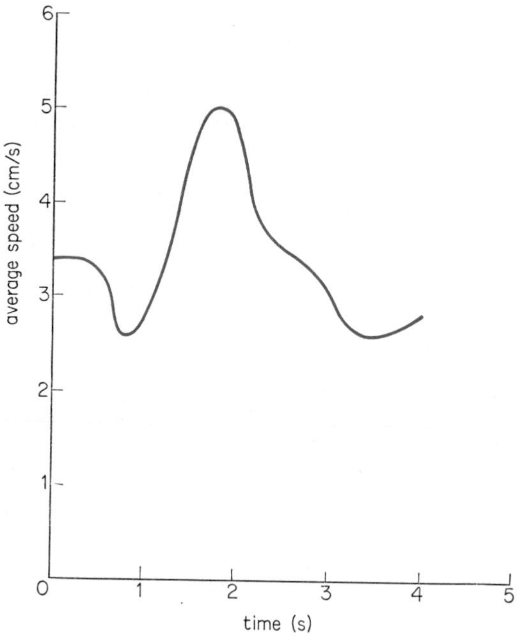

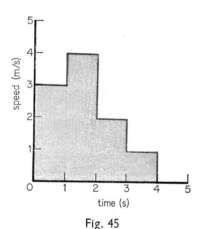

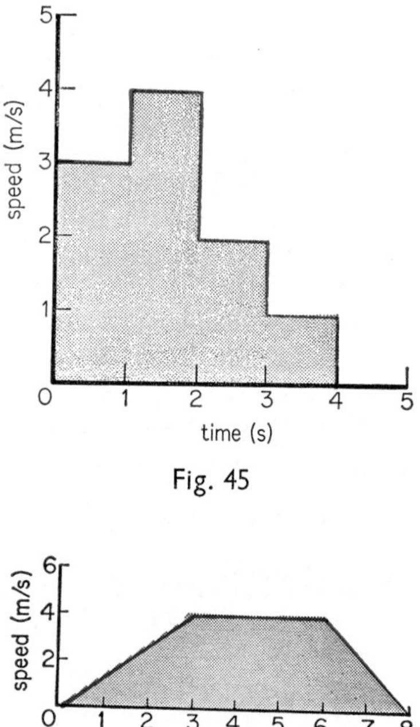

Fig. 45

Fig. 46

Fig. 43

In one second the body moves 4 metres. This is represented by the area A under the line PQ. In two seconds the body will move 8 metres. This may be represented by the areas A + B, that is, the area under PR. Similarly the distance gone after 3 seconds is given by the area A + B + C (= 12 m), and after 4 seconds by the area A + B + C + D (= 16 m).

If the areas A, B, C and D represent lengths of ticker tape, we see that the distance gone is proportional to the amount of tape which has passed through the timer.

Fig. 45 represents the speed of a body during 4 seconds. The graph shows the average speed during each second. *Find the distance gone in each of the 4 seconds and the total distance gone by the end of the fourth second.* (16) *What is the average speed during the 4 seconds?* (17)

Fig. 46 represents the speed of a cyclist during 8 seconds. How far did he travel during the first 3 seconds. (18) *What was the total distance gone?* (19) *What was his average speed during the 8 seconds?* (20)

Optional Extras

Frame of Reference

If you walk along the corridor of a train at 4 mi/h (relative to the carriage) and the train is travelling at 10 mi/h (relative to the Earth) your speed *relative to the Earth* might be 14 mi/h or it might be 6 mi/h. *When would it be 6 mi/h?* (21)

The speed of an aircraft may be quoted as air speed. *What does this mean?* (22) *Why is this not necessarily the same as the speed of the plane relative to the Earth?* (23) *What frame of reference is being used when dealing with air speed?* (24)

Although we will usually be thinking of the Earth's surface as our frame of reference we will have to consider cases in which other frames are used. If an elephant is tramping along, swinging its trunk from side to side while a fly walks calmly along the elephant's trunk, the fly's speed would most easily be considered relative to the trunk!

Speed and Velocity

How does the valve on a bicycle wheel move as you cycle along a level road? The following demonstration indicates one way of answering this problem.

Project 3.4. Paint the end of a cylindrical tin can matt black. Then paint a white *spot* near the rim to represent the valve of the bicycle wheel, and a small white *dot* at the centre to represent the hub of the wheel. Now place the can on a board which is tilted so that the can runs down the board at a constant speed (Fig. 47). Take a stroboscope picture of the end of the can as it runs down the slope. A suitable strobe speed is 5 pictures per second, that is, one slit of the strobe disc should be open.

Fig. 47

A photograph obtained from such an experiment is shown in Fig. 48. The white arrow indicates the direction in which the can was rolling. *What is our frame of reference in this photograph?* (25) *What can you say about the speed of the white spot relative to the board (Earth)?* (26) *Is the velocity of the white spot constant in the direction indicated by the arrow?* (27) *Does any part of the can move at constant velocity relative to the board?* (28) *How is this indicated on the photograph?* (29)

2

Let us return to the problem of the bicycle valve. We have seen how it moves relative to the Earth (Fig. 48). If, however, we could

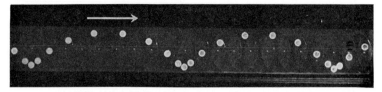

Fig. 48

Fig. 49

Fig. 50

mount a camera on the bicycle (Fig. 49) the photograph produced would show the motion of the valve *relative to the bicycle*. There is no need actually to do this experiment, which would be rather difficult, as we can produce a similar result by photographing a can rotating at a steady rate. The can shown in Fig. 47 was photographed as it rotated on a gramophone turntable.

If you imagine that Fig. 50 shows the motion of the valve relative to the bicycle (or the white spot relative to the centre of the can), you will see that its speed is now constant, as the distance between successive white spots on the photograph is the same in each case. *What is the frame of reference used in this photograph?* (30) *Is the velocity of the valve constant relative to the bicycle?* (31)

From these experiments we can see first that speed and velocity depend on the frame of reference. It is therefore important to be clear what particular frame of reference is being used. Secondly, we have seen that it is possible for a body to have a constant speed (for example, the valve relative to the bicycle), yet its velocity is changing all the time, because its direction is altering continuously.

Relative Velocity

Velocity is a vector quantity. Many problems relating to velocity can therefore be most easily solved using vector diagrams.

A boy and girl are standing at either end of a corridor in a train travelling at 100 mi/h. Suppose the boy is nearer the front of the train and throws a ball at 15 mi/h to the girl. If the ball doesn't slow down will the girl catch it at 115 mi/h, 85 mi/h or 15 mi/h? We can probably catch a glimpse here of one part of the 'Theory of Relativity', namely that 115 mi/h, 85 mi/h, and 15 mi/h have *no meaning by themselves*. It is usually obvious which frame of reference to use, but in this case it ought to be clearly stated, particularly as the Earth is not the only possible or even the most useful frame of reference.

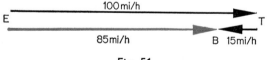

Fig. 51

If $\overrightarrow{ET}$ (Fig. 51) represents the velocity of the train with respect to the Earth and $\overleftarrow{BT}$ the velocity of the ball relative to the train, the resultant velocity of the ball relative to Earth is represented by

$\overrightarrow{\text{EB}}$. The ball, then, is travelling at 85 mi/h (forward) relative to the Earth, but from the girl's point of view the important velocity is its velocity *relative to her*. As she is travelling with the train and the ball is travelling at 15 mi/h (back) relative to the train, this will also be the velocity of the ball relative to the girl.

Imagine that a barge is slowly moving up a river with a velocity of 2 m/s relative to the river. A dog runs across the barge at 3 m/s and the river is flowing at 1 m/s (Fig. 52).

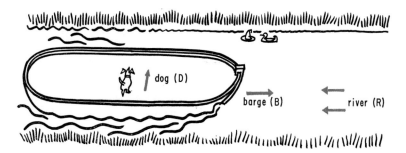

Fig. 52

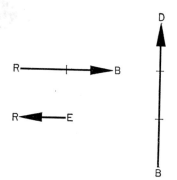

Fig. 53

The three velocities can be represented by the vectors shown in Fig. 53. We can join the three vectors together, and use the figure thus produced to find the dog's velocity (i) relative to the river and (ii) relative to the Earth. First we must join the vectors so that the B's and R's coincide (Fig. 54).

The red vector RD now indicates the velocity of the dog relative to the river, and the dotted red vector ED shows the dog's velocity relative to Earth. *Find the magnitudes of these velocities by two different methods and state the directions of the velocities, assuming that the river was flowing west.* (32)

Relativity

If you were on a space ship millions of miles from the nearest star or planet how would you know if you were at rest or moving at a constant velocity? No experiment would ever tell you the answer. You know how difficult it is to tell whether it is your train or the one next to you which is moving out of a station. Einstein is reputed to have asked at Euston 'Does Crewe stop at this train?'

You might like to discuss the following (unlikely) story!

A ship is just leaving a pier. As it moves away a man on board is speaking to his girl friend on the pier. He walks back along the ship so that he stays opposite the girl. When he knocks down an old lady he protests that he was really at rest and she was moving! (33)

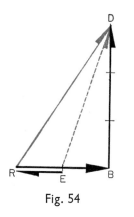

Fig. 54

Problems

34. *A jet plane flies south at a speed (relative to the air) of 600 mi/h. It is, however, blown west by a 100 mi/h wind. What is its velocity relative to the ground? Remember to state magnitude and direction.*

35.   *State* (i) *what is measured by each of the following quantities, and* (ii) *which are vector quantities?*

> (a) *300 miles*
> (b) *300 metres* (west)
> (c) *20 mi/h* (east)
> (d) *4 metres/second*
> (e) *10 kgf* (down)
> (f) 4×10^3 *kg*

36.   *The minute hand of a clock is 10 cm long. Find the displacement and average velocity of its tip* (i) *between 5.00 and 5.15* (ii) *between 10.00 and 11.00 and* (iii) *between 1.30 and 2.15.*

37.   *A car travels west at 40 mi/h for 30 minutes and then south at 30 mi/h for 30 minutes. How far did it travel? What was its displacement? Find its average speed and its average velocity.*

38.   *A cyclist goes north at 15 mi/h for 10 miles and then east at 20 mi/h for 10 miles. Find his average speed and his average velocity.*

39.   *ABCD is a square, each side being 100 metres long. A man walks east from A to B and then south to C. Finally he runs to D, where he arrives two minutes after leaving A. Find* (i) *the distance he travelled* (ii) *his displacement* (iii) *his average velocity and* (iv) *his average speed.*

40.   *A canoe is being paddled upstream at 2·5 m/s relative to the river which is flowing east at 1·5 m/s. If an Indian on the canoe shoots an arrow due north at 15 m/s, relative to the canoe, find the velocity of the arrow relative to the Earth.*

41.   *A racing car travels 10 miles east at 400 mi/h assisted by a tail wind. On his return trip west the driver clocks only 300 mi/h. Find his average speed and his average velocity.*

42.   *How long will a satellite take to circle the Earth if it travels at 8×10^3 m/s in a circular orbit of radius $7·6 \times 10^6$ m?*

Visual Aids

8 mm Cassettes: The velocity vector[18] 80-252.
16 mm Films: Vectors (P.S.S.C.)[26] 3D.2684.

Acceleration

CHAPTER 4

Stepping on the Gas

If you were sitting on the pillion seat of a powerful motor bike accelerating along a straight road, you might not feel inclined to record the speedometer reading every second. *Can you think how a cine camera, taking 18 pictures every second, might be used to obtain this information?* (1) Let us assume, then, that we can obtain speedometer readings every second and that they are as follows.

Time	0	1	2	3	4	5	6	7	8	seconds
Speed	0	$7\frac{1}{2}$	15	$22\frac{1}{2}$	30	$37\frac{1}{2}$	45	$52\frac{1}{2}$	60	mi/h

By how much has the speed increased every second? This could be expressed as an acceleration of $7\frac{1}{2}$ mi/h per second. *Draw a graph showing how the speed varies with time.* (2)

In practice the speed of a motor cycle or car does not usually increase in this uniform way. The power of the engine is not constant at all speeds. The friction in the bearings varies and the air resistance increases with speed. Changing gears also prevents uniform acceleration of the kind illustrated in your graph. In practice, the graph might look more like that shown in Fig. 55.

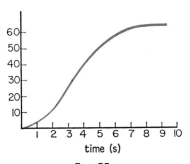

Fig. 55

Between what speeds is the acceleration shown in Fig. 55 almost constant? (3) *What happens after 8 seconds of acceleration?* (4)

Miles per hour, per second

$7\frac{1}{2}$ mi/h can be expressed in feet per second as follows

$$7\frac{1}{2} \text{ mi/h} = 7\frac{1}{2} \times 5280 \text{ feet per hour}$$

$$= 7\frac{1}{2} \times \frac{5280}{60 \times 60} \text{ feet per second}$$

$$= 11 \text{ feet per second}$$

An acceleration of $7\frac{1}{2}$ mi/h per second could then equally well be written as 11 ft/s per second. This means that the speed is increasing by 11 ft/s every second. We will write this as 11 ft/s/s or 11 ft/s².

Uniform acceleration in a straight line

Acceleration can be measured in miles per hour per second (mi/h/s) or feet per second per second (ft/s²), but we will normally express acceleration in metric units, for example, metres per second per second (m/s²). The graph in Fig. 56 represents uniform acceleration in which the speed increases by two metres per second per second. The acceleration is, therefore, 2 metres per second

29

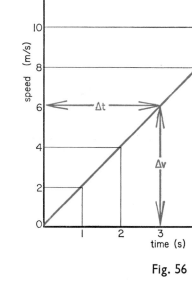

speed/time graph

Fig. 56

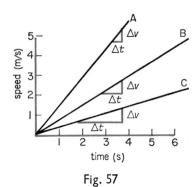

Fig. 57

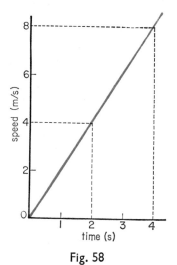

Fig. 58

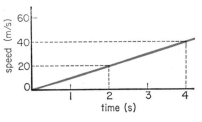

Fig. 59

per second (2 m/s²). This can be found by considering any change of speed (Δv) and dividing by the time (Δt) during which this change of speed took place.

Acceleration is defined as the change of *velocity* per unit time interval, but, as we are dealing with straight line motion, we need only consider the change in the magnitude of velocity with time, that is, the change of speed with time.

We have:

$$\text{acceleration} = \frac{\text{change of speed}}{\text{time taken}}$$

$$= \frac{\Delta v}{\Delta t}$$

$$= \frac{6 \text{ m/s}}{3 \text{ s}}$$

$$= 2 \text{ m/s}^2$$

Slope

The change of speed (Δv) divided by the corresponding change in time (Δt) is called the *gradient* or *slope* of the graph. If the speed, time scales are the same, as in Fig. 57, the steeper the graph is the greater will be its slope. A has a greater slope than B, and B a greater slope than C.

If, however, two graphs have different speed/time scales, as in Figs. 58 and 59, the steeper line does not necessarily have a greater *slope*.

In Fig. 58 a steep line represents

$$\frac{\Delta v}{\Delta t} = \frac{8}{4} = 2 \text{ m/s}^2$$

whereas in Fig. 59 a less steep line represents

$$\frac{\Delta v}{\Delta t} = \frac{40}{4} = 10 \text{ m/s}^2$$

From the second graph we see that in the same time interval there is five times the change in speed. As $\frac{\Delta v}{\Delta t}$ is greater in the second graph it is said to have a greater *slope*.

Problem 5. Calculate from Fig. 58 how far the body travelled in 1, 2, 3 and 4 seconds. How far did it travel in the first, second, third and fourth seconds? Is there any simple way in which the distance travelled in one second is related to the distance travelled during the next second?

Experiment 4.1. Attach a length of tape to a trolley$_{3,6}$ and allow it to run down a sloping track (Fig. 60). By passing the tape

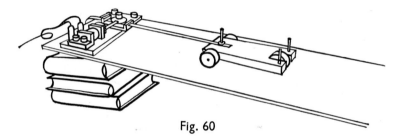

Fig. 60

through a timer the speed of the trolley at various times can be found. As the dots produced on the tape will be very crowded at the beginning of the movement, ignore the first few and then cut the tape into lengths of (say) 10 spaces. If the timer produces 50 dots per second, each length of tape will indicate the distance gone in one fifth of a second, that is, it represents the average speed over that time interval. Paste the lengths of tape, in order, on a piece of graph paper as shown in Fig. 61.

The centre of the top of each strip (red dot) represents the average speed during one fifth of a second. If all the dots lie more or less in a straight line the trolley has moved with uniform acceleration. Draw a straight line with your ruler so that it will pass as close as possible to each dot and work from this.

Using the numbers shown in Fig. 61 we see that the speed has increased from 2 cm/$\frac{1}{5}$ s to 7 cm/$\frac{1}{5}$ s in one second. The acceleration can be found as follows.

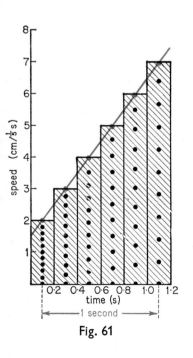

Fig. 61

$$\text{acceleration} = \frac{\text{change in speed}}{\text{time taken}}$$

$$= \frac{(7-2) \text{ cm/}\frac{1}{5}\text{ s}}{1 \text{ second}}$$

$$= 5 \text{ (cm/}\frac{1}{5} \text{ sec) per second}$$

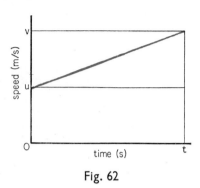

Fig. 62

If a trolley travels 5 cm in one fifth of a second it will, if the speed is maintained, cover 25 cm in one second. A speed of 5 cm/$\frac{1}{5}$ s is therefore equal to a speed of 25 cm/s, and the trolley accelerates at 25 cm/s per second or 25 cm/s².

From the graph you can also see that the speed increases by 1 centimetre per fifth of a second per fifth of a second, so that

$$1 \text{ cm}/\tfrac{1}{5}\text{ s}/\tfrac{1}{5}\text{ s} = 25 \text{ cm/s/s or } 25 \text{ cm/s}^2$$

The graph used in Experiment 4.1 can be drawn as shown in Fig. 62.

Here u stands for the speed when we start timing. This is sometimes called 'initial speed'. v stands for the speed at the end of the timing period. It is sometimes called 'final speed'. Note that 'initial' and 'final' in this connection do not mean the start and finish of the movement, but rather the start and finish of the timing. The body may be in motion before the 'initial speed' is measured, and still moving after the 'final speed' is reached.

If t is the time taken for the speed to increase from u to v we have:

$$\text{acceleration} = \frac{\text{change in speed}}{\text{time taken for change}}$$

$$= \frac{v - u}{t}$$

speed at end of timing period (m/s)

speed at beginning of timing period (m/s)

$$a = \frac{v - u}{t}$$

time for change of speed to occur (s)

acceleration (m/s²)

This and the other equations we shall use for acceleration apply only to *uniform acceleration along a straight path*.

Problems

6. *Can you find an expression for the final speed (v) of an object which was moving at **u** m/s before being accelerated at **a** m/s² for t seconds? What is the speed of a body which is accelerated from rest at **a** m/s² for t seconds?*

7. *A train travelling at 10 m/s accelerates to 20 m/s in 5 seconds. Find its acceleration. What will be its speed after a further 3 seconds if it continues to accelerate at the same rate?*

8. *A cyclist starting from rest accelerates at 2 m/s² for 3 seconds. What is his final speed? A car travelling at 20 m/s comes to rest in 5 seconds. Find its acceleration. Is it positive or negative?*

In the last problem the acceleration is found to be *negative*. This means the car is slowing down. A negative acceleration is sometimes referred to as a *retardation* or *deceleration*.

9. *A body moving with a speed of 20 m/s is decelerated uniformly at 5 m/s². Find its speed after 2, 4 and then 6 seconds of such deceleration.*

10. *If a rocket, starting from rest, reaches a speed of 34,560 km/h in 2 minutes find its average acceleration in m/s².*

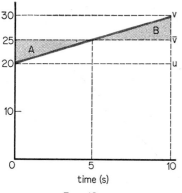

time (s)

Fig. 63

Average Speed During Uniform Acceleration

If you go 90 miles in 3 hours your average speed is 30 mi/h. That is, you would cover the same distance in the same time if you maintained a constant speed of 30 mi/h.

If a body accelerates uniformly from 20 m/s to 30 m/s in 10 seconds (Fig. 63), the total displacement is indicated by the area below the red line. If now we draw a horizontal line at 25 m/s thus forming two congruent triangles A and B, the area below this line must be exactly the same as the area below the red line. *Why?*

25 m/s is therefore that constant speed at which the body must travel to cover the same distance (area of rectangle) in the same time (10 seconds). *When, during its period of acceleration, was the body moving at 25 m/s, its average speed?* (11) To find the average speed ($\bar{v}$) we add together 20 (i.e. *u*) and 30 (i.e. *v*) and divide by 2.

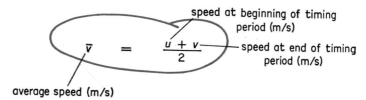

speed at beginning of timing period (m/s)

$$\bar{v} = \frac{u + v}{2}$$

speed at end of timing period (m/s)

average speed (m/s)

Note: This method of finding the average speed of a body can be used only for uniform acceleration.

Problem 12. A ball accelerates uniformly from rest until it is falling at 40 m/s. What is its average speed? If its acceleration was 10 m/s², how long did it take to reach (a) 20 m/s (b) 40 m/s? If it continued to fall with the same acceleration after reaching 40 m/s, how far would it fall during the next second?

Uniform acceleration from rest

If the acceleration of a body is constant its *change of speed* (Δv) is the same every second.

If a body moves from rest with a constant acceleration of *a* m/s² its

speed at the end of 1 second is *a*   m/s
speed at the end of 2 seconds is *a* × 2 m/s
speed at the end of 3 seconds is *a* × 3 m/s
speed at the end of *t* seconds is *a* × *t* m/s

$$v = at \quad . \quad . \quad . \quad . \quad . \quad (1)$$

As the average speed $\bar{v} = \dfrac{u + v}{2}$

$$\bar{v} = \frac{0 + at}{2} = \frac{at}{2}$$

The distance gone = average speed × time

hence $d = \dfrac{at}{2} \times t$

$s = \frac{1}{2} at^2$

$$d = \tfrac{1}{2} at^2 \quad . \quad . \quad . \quad . \quad . \quad (2)$$

The same result can be found by considering the area under the graph in Fig. 64.

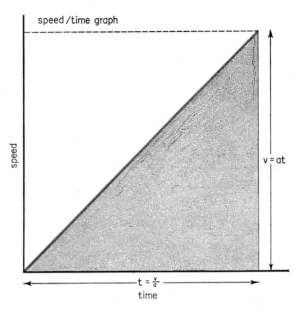

Fig. 64

After t seconds from rest the speed $= at$, so that the distance is equal to the area of the shaded triangle.

$$\text{distance gone} = \tfrac{1}{2} vt \quad . \quad . \quad . \quad . \quad (3)$$

$$\text{or } d = \tfrac{1}{2} (at) t$$

$s = \tfrac{1}{2} at^2$
$$d = \tfrac{1}{2} at^2 \quad . \quad . \quad . \quad . \quad (2)$$

The distance can also be expressed in terms of the speed and acceleration. As $t = \dfrac{v}{a}$ we have:

$$\text{distance gone} = \tfrac{1}{2} vt$$

$$= \tfrac{1}{2} v \left(\frac{v}{a} \right)$$

$s = \dfrac{v^2}{2a}$
$$d = \frac{v^2}{2a} \quad . \quad . \quad . \quad . \quad (4)$$

Equation 2 shows that the distance gone is directly proportional to the square of the time, and equation 4 shows that it is directly proportional to the square of the speed. A first look at equation might lead you to think that d is directly proportional to t. *Why is this not so?* (13) (Hint: can you find an expression for v?).

There is no need to memorise all four equations. Equation 3 can be deduced from a speed/time graph, and equation 1 is simply th definition of acceleration. You might, however, find it useful to remember the other equations as follows.

$s = at^2$

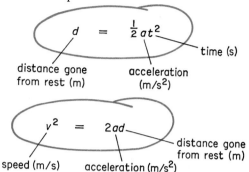

$v^2 = 2as$

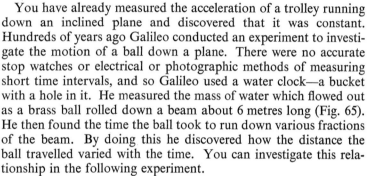

Galileo's Inclined Plane

Fig. 65

You have already measured the acceleration of a trolley running down an inclined plane and discovered that it was constant. Hundreds of years ago Galileo conducted an experiment to investigate the motion of a ball down a plane. There were no accurate stop watches or electrical or photographic methods of measuring short time intervals, and so Galileo used a water clock—a bucket with a hole in it. He measured the mass of water which flowed out as a brass ball rolled down a beam about 6 metres long (Fig. 65). He then found the time the ball took to run down various fractions of the beam. By doing this he discovered how the distance the ball travelled varied with the time. You can investigate this relationship in the following experiment.

Experiment 4.2. Two 3 metre lengths of Dexion Speedframe, placed side by side, and held together with Sellotape at the ends, form an excellent beam down which to roll a large ball bearing.

Construct a pendulum or adjust a metronome so that it ticks seconds. Now allow the ball to start moving down the track on one of the ticks, and mark its position with chalk at successive ticks. In this way you can find the distance gone by the ball during each second. Allow the ball to run down the slope again, and check that the marks are in the correct places. Measure the distances travelled by the ball during each second, and then calculate how much further the ball rolled during one second compared with the previous second; that is, find the extra distance gone each second.

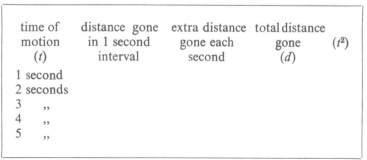

time of motion (t)	distance gone in 1 second interval	extra distance gone each second	total distance gone (d)	(t^2)
1 second				
2 seconds				
3 ,,				
4 ,,				
5 ,,				

What do your results suggest?

Now calculate the total distance gone (*d*) from the start after each second and the square of the time (*t²*). Are these quantities related? What does this mean? Does this confirm your original analysis of the results?

An interesting alternative can be devised using a flywheel-driven toy car running down an inclined board. The distances covered in equal time intervals can then be chalked on the board. As the car moves relatively slowly a stop watch is adequate for the timing.

Problems

14. *A tape, produced by a trolley moving down a sloping runway, is marked off in groups of 10-tick lengths starting at a point where the dots can be clearly distinguished. If the distances from this*

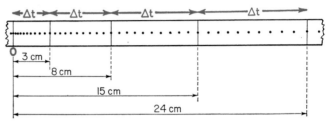

Fig. 66

point are as shown in Fig. 66, complete the following table, assuming that the timer was producing 10 dots per second (i.e. Δt = 1 second).

Distance from 0 (*d*)	Average speed during time interval $\bar{v} = \dfrac{\Delta d}{\Delta t}$	Acceleration during time interval $a = \dfrac{\Delta v}{\Delta t}$
0 cm		
3 cm		
8 cm		
15 cm		
24 cm		

15. *A car is left standing on a hill (an inclined plane). Suddenly the brake cable snaps and the car careers straight down the hill, reaching a speed of 5 m/s after travelling 10 m. How much farther would it travel before reaching 10 m/s, assuming it continues to accelerate at the same rate? What is the acceleration?*

16. *A toy car travels from rest down a sloping board, covering each of the following distances in 4 second intervals: 20 cm, 60 cm, 100 cm, 140 cm. Does this represent constant acceleration? If so, what is the acceleration?*

17. *If a body accelerates from rest at 3 m/s² for 3 minutes, what is its final speed? How far has it gone? What is its average speed during these 3 minutes? When was its instantaneous speed equal to*

its average speed? What was the speed of the body after it had trav-elled the first 600 m? How long did it take to travel that distance?

18. *A cyclist starts from rest and accelerates at 1 m/s² for 10 seconds. He then travels at a constant speed for 20 seconds and finally decelerates at 2 m/s² until he stops. Draw a speed/time graph and use it to calculate the total distance gone. What was his average speed during his times of acceleration and deceleration? What was his maximum speed?*

Measuring Constant Acceleration

If we know that a body is *accelerating uniformly* there are various short-cuts for finding the value of the acceleration. We discovered that a trolley or a ball moving down an inclined plane accelerated at a uniform rate. To find such an acceleration all we would have to do would be to measure the time taken for a body to travel a known distance from rest. As $d = \frac{1}{2} at^2$ the acceleration can then be calculated. It is $2\dfrac{d}{t^2}$.

As it is not always possible to measure the time taken for a body to move a certain distance from rest, we will often use the following method based on the definition of acceleration, that is, the change of speed per unit of time.

Imagine a car travelling at 10 mi/h and accelerating uniformly (Fig. 67). Four seconds later it is travelling at 50 mi/h. Its acceleration may be found as follows:

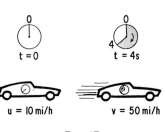

$$\text{acceleration} = \frac{v - u}{t}$$

$$= \frac{50 - 10 \text{ mi/h}}{4 \text{ s}}$$

$$= \frac{40 \text{ mi/h}}{4 \text{ s}}$$

$$= 10 \text{ mi/h/s}$$

Fig. 67

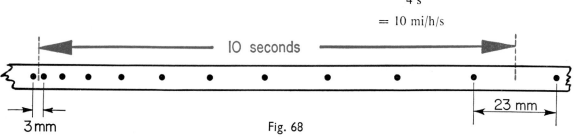

Fig. 68

Fig. 68 represents a piece of tape pulled through a timer by a trolley running down an inclined plane. For simplicity let us imagine that the timer makes one dot per second. We will select a convenient 'initial' speed $(u) = 3$ mm/s and a 'final' speed $(v) = 23$ mm/s. Then the

$$\text{change in speed} = v - u$$
$$= 23 - 3$$
$$= 20 \text{ mm/s}$$

The time taken for this change to take place may be found by counting the number of one second intervals from the 3 mm space to the 23 mm space. In this case it is 10 seconds. Then

$$\text{acceleration} = \frac{v - u}{t}$$

$$= \frac{20}{10}$$

$$= 2\cdot 0 \text{ mm/s}^2$$

In practice the timer is more likely to produce (say) 50 dots per second. If the above tape had been marked by such a timer the result would be

$$2\cdot 0 \text{ mm}/\tfrac{1}{50} \text{ s per } \tfrac{1}{50} \text{ second}$$

$$= 2\cdot 0 \times 50 \text{ mm/s per } \tfrac{1}{50} \text{ second}$$

$$= 100 \text{ mm/s per } \tfrac{1}{50} \text{ second}$$

$$= 100 \times 50 \text{ mm/s per second}$$

$$= 5000 \text{ mm/s}^2$$

$$= 5\cdot 0 \text{ m/s}^2$$

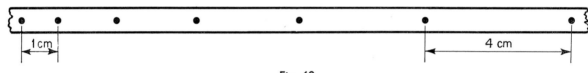

1 cm   4 cm

Fig. 69

Problem 19. *If the tape illustrated in Fig. 69 was made by a body moving with constant acceleration and a dot was produced every twentieth of a second, find the acceleration of the body in metres per second per second.*

If Fig. 70 represents a stroboscopic photograph of a ball running down a plane, we can calculate the acceleration using the same

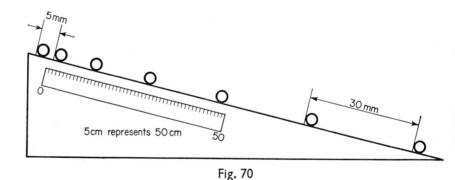

5 mm

30 mm

5 cm represents 50 cm   50

Fig. 70

method. The 'initial' speed (u) can be found by measuring the distance between two adjacent images. In this case we have chosen two images 5 mm apart. Our 'final' speed (v) is found from two images 30 mm apart. If we call the time between flashes 'one tick', the speeds can be written

$$u = 5 \text{ mm/tick}$$

$$v = 30 \text{ mm/tick}$$

Change of speed

$$= v - u$$

$$= 30 - 5$$

$$= 25 \text{ mm/tick}$$

As the ball took 5 ticks for its speed to increase from 5 mm/tick to 30 mm/tick, the acceleration may be found as follows.

$$\text{acceleration} = \frac{v - u}{t}$$

$$= \frac{25}{5}$$

$$= 5 \text{ mm/tick/tick}$$

Although for some purposes an answer of this kind is sufficient, you may want to calculate the acceleration of the ball in (say) metres/second/second. To do this you must know
(a) the scale of the photograph, and
(b) the length of a 'tick' in seconds.
The scale may be found by including a $\frac{1}{2}$ metre stick in the photograph. In this case the image of the $\frac{1}{2}$ metre stick measures 5 cm, thus giving the scale as 5 to 50 or 1 to 10.
The length of a 'tick' can be found from the stroboscope dial or from the number of openings per second of the shutter. In Fig. 70 there are 5 flashes per second giving

$$1 \text{ 'tick'} = \tfrac{1}{5} \text{ second}$$

Substituting these values in our results we see that on the photograph

$$5 \text{ mm/tick/tick}$$

$$\text{represents } 5 \times 10 \text{ mm/tick/tick}$$

$$= 5 \text{ cm}/\tfrac{1}{5} \text{ s}/\tfrac{1}{5} \text{ s}$$

$$= (5 \times 5 \text{ cm/s}) \text{ per } \tfrac{1}{5} \text{ s}$$

$$= 5 \times 5 \times 5 \text{ cm/s/s}$$

$$= 1\cdot25 \text{ m/s/s or } 1\cdot25 \text{ m/s}^2$$

Problem 20. *Fig. 71 shows a vehicle moving down an almost friction-free air track. The photographs were taken every tenth of a second, and a half metre stick has been photographed below the apparatus. Find the acceleration of the vehicle in metres per second per second.*

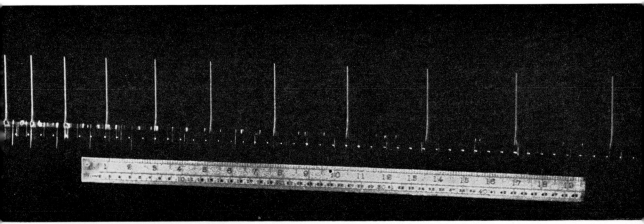

Fig. 71

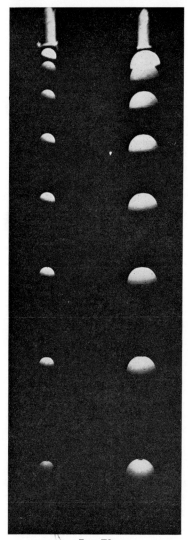

Fig. 72

Free Fall

Aristotle taught that heavy bodies fell faster than light ones. A 100 kg mass would fall 100 m in the time taken for a 1 kg mass to fall 1 m. The Dutch scientist, Stevinus, conducted an experiment in 1586 which showed that this was false. He dropped spheres which had different masses and showed that they fell at practically the same rate. Galileo, so legend has it, conducted a similar experiment. As we have the advantage of using electro-magnets and stroboscopic photography—denied to Galileo—we can construct a similar experiment quickly and simply without climbing Pisa's Tower!

Demonstration 4.3. Insert iron screws into two wooden spheres. One sphere should have a different mass from the other. The spheres have to be held by two electro-magnets connected to the same circuit so that they can be released at the same instant. Pieces of Sellotape attached to each core often ensure rapid release.

The photograph in Fig. 72 was taken using two white-painted spheres. They were released together and a strobe photograph taken at 20 flashes per second.

Do they fall with different accelerations? Are their accelerations constant? Would a feather and a ball give the same results? Explain your answer (Book 1, page 94).

Galileo realised that there was a very, very slight difference in the times taken by different spheres to fall a given distance. Can you suggest a reason for the difference? As it was not then possible to produce a good vacuum, Galileo guessed that if there were no air present the spheres would fall at exactly the same rate.

Experiment 4.4. Using a mains-operated timer, which produces 50 dotes each second, you can investigate the motion of a 1 kg mass falling under gravity (Fig. 7e). Admittedly there is a little friction because of the timer, but it is small compared with the force of gravity exerted on the mass.

Find, from the tape, if the acceleration is constant. What is the value of the acceleration in meters per second per second?

Experiment 4.5. Drop a ball bearing through at least 5 metres and time the fall with a stop watch. Calculate the acceleration of gravity in metres per second per second, assuming that (*a*) there is no air resistance and (*b*) the acceleration is constant. Discuss the accuracy of this method.

Experiment 4.6. To find the acceleration of gravity with precision it is necessary to use a very accurate timing device. Either an electric stop clock$_{2,9}$ or a scaler$_8$ with a built-in oscillator is suitable for such a determination. Arrange the circuit so that when a ball bearing is released from an electro-magnet it breaks the circuit and

Fig. 73

Fig. 74

starts the timer (Fig. 74). When it strikes a small 'trap door', which is held closed magnetically, it breaks another circuit and so stops the clock. Use this apparatus to find the time taken for the ball to fall through six different distances. Calculate the accelerations each time, and hence find the average value for the six readings.

The acceleration of gravity varies over the Earth's surface. In Britain it is approximately 9·8 m/s².

Project 4.7. Tie pieces of metal, preferably lead, to a length of string at intervals of (say) 10 cm, 30 cm, 50 cm, 70 cm and 90 cm (Fig. 75). Release the string and explain what you hear.

The well of a staircase is particularly suitable for this experiment.

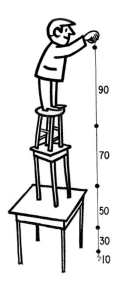

Fig. 75

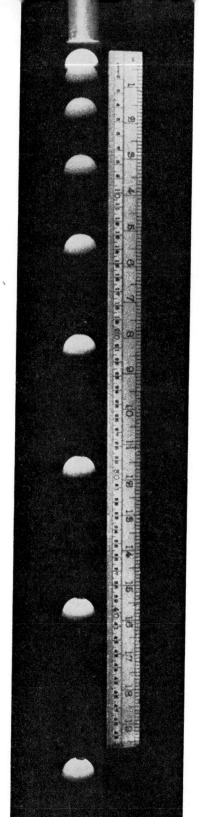

Fig. 76

Problems

21. *Fig. 76 shows a ball bearing falling freely under gravity. The ball was illuminated by a stroboscope producing 25 flashes per second, and the stick at the side of the photograph is 50 centimetres long. Find the acceleration of the ball bearing.*

22. *If a stone dropped from the Empire State Building took 9·6 seconds to reach the ground, how high is the building? How fast would the stone be falling when it hit the ground? Ignore air resistance in both cases.*

23. *An arrow is shot at 30 m/s vertically upwards. Assuming the gravitational acceleration is 10 m/s² and ignoring air resistance, find (a) how high it will rise, (b) how long it will take to reach that height and (c) how long it will take to fall back from its maximum height to the Earth.*

Project 4.8. (a) You can use your knowledge of the acceleration of gravity to find the reaction time of a friend.

Attach a large ball bearing to an electro-magnet fixed near the top of a metre stick as shown in Fig. 77. Ask your friend to place

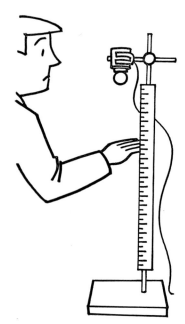

Fig. 77

his hand under the ball and to jerk it away as soon as he sees the ball starting to fall. The switch for the electro-magnet should be out of sight.

How near to the ball can your friend bring his hand without being hit? Calculate, from this distance, your friend's reaction time.

(b) Can you find your reaction time by another method in which your friend drops a metre stick? The stick should first be held vertically against a wall and as it falls you stop the stick by pressing it against the wall. Remember that displacement is given by $\frac{1}{2} at^2$.

Summary of equations used in this chapter

Write down each of the following equations, stating what each letter represents and what units are used in the international system (24).

$$v = u + at$$

$$\bar{v} = \frac{u + v}{2}$$

$$v^2 = 2as$$

$$v^2 = 2\,ad$$

$$s = \tfrac{1}{2}at^2$$

$$d = \tfrac{1}{2}\,at^2$$

*In the first equation what does **at** represent? (25)*
We could re-write the third equation as

$$d = \frac{v}{2} \times \frac{v}{a}$$

What would $\frac{v}{2}$ and $\frac{v}{a}$ represent? (26)

In the last equation what does $\frac{at}{2}$ represent? (27)

Newton 1—Definition of a Force

CHAPTER 5

Mass, Measurement and Motion

What is a definition? Dr Johnson once defined a network as 'anything reticulated or decussated with interstices between the intersections!' Some dictionary definitions are not very much more enlightening. For example, one dictionary defines a cow as the 'female of the bull', and a bull as the 'male of the cow'. When you were very young a cow was probably any large hairy creature with a leg at each corner. Later you learned to distinguish calves, cows, bulls, and bullocks, and if you are seriously interested you can probably recognise Ayrshires, Friesians, Herefords, Jerseys and Belted Galloways.

In physics, too, we often begin with vague ideas and gradually change to more precise definitions as we learn more about the subject. In your first year, for example, *mass* was the amount of stuff in a body and *force* a push or a pull. In this section we will develop these ideas so that we can measure mass and force.

Earlier in this course we found that temperature could not be measured directly, and so we had to look for something which depended on temperature and which *could* be measured. We discovered that the volume of a liquid, such as mercury, varied with the temperature, and so we measured the volume of mercury in order to find the temperature.

If we are going to measure mass we must look for some property of mass which can easily be measured. You have already used the pull of gravity on a body as a measure of its mass. We assumed that the force (weight) was proportional to the quantity of matter (mass). Twice the weight meant twice the mass, thrice the weight thrice the mass, and so on. Later we will see that this assumption is perfectly valid.

Suppose, however, that you were in a space ship in which no gravitational pull could be detected. *Could we use a beam balance or a spring balance to find the weight (and hence the mass) of a body?* (1) *If it had no weight would it have no mass?* (2) In our space-ship we must look for another way of measuring mass. *What other properties does mass have?* (3)

Experiment 5.1. Ask a friend to knock a small tack into a piece of wood placed on top of a pile of books on your head (Fig. 78). Why does this not hurt you?

Fig. 78

In the first year you tried pushing an empty can suspended by a long string (Book 1, p. 100), and then you pushed a similar can filled with metal or sand. *Which was more easily moved?* (4) *Was this because of greater air resistance or greater gravitational pull on the other?* (5) *If a cyclist and a 10-ton lorry, each travelling at*

44

30 mi/h, run into a wall, which does the greater damage to the wall? (6)   Why? (7)   Would you prefer to kick a football or a stone of the same size? (8)   Why? (9)

This unwillingness to get moving or, once moving, to stop, is called *inertia*. It comes from the Latin word for laziness! The greater the mass of a body the greater its inertia, and so we can use this property of mass to measure mass.

Experiment 5.2. Place a trolley on a level board. Attach one end of a stretched spring to the trolley and hold the other end of the spring stationary. Watch the acceleration of the trolley.

Now load the trolley with a brick, or several other trolleys, and see if its acceleration is altered when the same spring is used as before.

By using 2 springs, as in the next experiment, this 'resistance to acceleration' can be investigated in terms of the period of oscillation.

Experiment 5.3. Connect a 1-foot length of $\frac{1}{4}$ in steel spring (22 gauge) to one end of a trolley$_6$ which is standing in the middle of a level board. Attach the other end of the spring to a pin fixed to the board or to a retort stand. Attach a similar spring to the other end of a trolley, as shown in Fig. 79. Now move the trolley

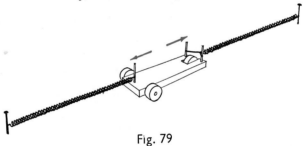

Fig. 79

in one direction and release it so that it oscillates backwards and forwards. Use a stop watch to find the period of oscillation, that is, one complete to and fro movement. Do you measure only *one* oscillation?

Repeat this experiment with two, three and four identical trolleys stacked on top of one another, and plot on a graph the period against the mass, assuming the mass of each trolley is the same. How would you test that each of the trolleys has the same mass?

Now attach a brick to one trolley and find the period of oscillation. From your graph determine the mass of the brick plus trolley. Taking a trolley as the 'unit of mass' find the mass of the brick. Now find the mass of a trolley and the brick by weighing them, and see how your results compare with those obtained by the above method.

Does this method of measuring mass depend on gravity? Could you conduct this experiment on a space ship out in empty space?

Experiment 5.4. (*a*) The wig-wag machine$_3$ (Fig. 80) is another type of inertial balance. Use clamps or metal cylinders as units of mass and plot the vibration time (period) against the number of cylinders in the tray. Does this device depend on the weight of the cylinders?

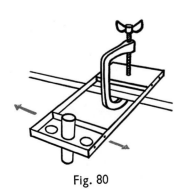

Fig. 80

(b) Lay two cylinders in the tray and place a powerful magnet below them so that the downwards force is increased. Does this affect the period of oscillation? Would the magnet affect the 'weight' as indicated on a spring balance?

(c) Repeat the original experiment, using only one cylinder, but now *remove* the vertical force on the tray by supporting the cylinder on a long string. Does this affect the period of oscillation?

The apparatus used in each of the above experiments is called an *inertial balance*. It measures the inertia of a body—the most fundamental property of mass. The terms inertia, mass and inertial mass are in fact often used to describe the same thing. Before we can measure mass we must first define a unit of mass. Bricks and clamps are hardly suitable as universal units of mass! *What is taken as the standard unit of mass?* (10) *What is it made of?* (11) *Where is it kept?* (12) Having fixed this standard it is possible to find the mass, in kilograms, of any other object by using an inertial balance, whose operation is not affected by gravity or its absence.

For practical purposes, however, it is much simpler to use a spring, lever or beam balance rather than an inertial balance in order to find the mass of an object. The gravitational pull (weight) is proportional to the mass (inertia) at any given point on the Earth. In 1922 Eotvos, using a delicate torsion balance, showed this proportionality to be correct to within 1 part in 200 million!

Aristotle and Common Sense

In his 'Mechanics' Aristotle said that 'a moving body comes to a standstill when the force which pushes it along can no longer so act as to push it'. It is hardly surprising that for 2,000 years this doctrine was accepted, considering that it describes what happens in our everyday experience. Try pushing a box, a bicycle or a ball. Each will stop soon after you stop pushing it. Try pushing a wooden block along a rough bench, a polished bench and a bench covered with polystyrene beads. *Can you explain the differences observed?* (13) Whenever we try to move something we meet with opposition. *How is the effect of friction reduced in machines?* (14) *How are the effects of air resistance minimised in cars and air-craft?* (15)

As the Aristotelians believed that a constant force kept things moving at a constant speed, they thought that an increasing force was needed for acceleration. They knew that a falling body accelerates, and so to explain this they said that the pull increases as the body approaches the Earth's surface.

Practical Puzzle 16. Consider the experiment illustrated in Fig. 81. If two identical masses are connected by a long string passing over a pulley as shown, the lower mass always moves downwards. Does this prove that there is a greater force pulling the lower mass? Use a spring balance to weigh the masses at these two positions. Explain your results.

So strong was the belief that a force was needed to keep a body moving, that various strange theories were invented to account for

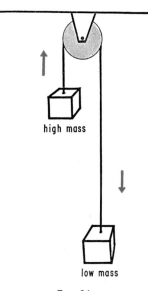

high mass

low mass

Fig. 81

the fact that a stone continued to move through the air after it had left the thrower's hand. Aristotle himself claimed that the motion of the hand caused the air to move and this moving air continued to waft the stone along. *If this were true could things move in a vacuum?* (17) To answer this difficulty Aristotle asserted that a vacuum couldn't exist!

A later theory stated that the air in front of the stone parted and closed up behind the body, so pushing it along. Later still, Francis Bacon said that the stone moved because of its elasticity. When the stone was pushed the back of the stone was compressed. This compression was passed on along the stone to the front thus keeping it moving.

Galileo and Gravity

Galileo challenged many of the beliefs of Aristotle and his followers and in particular their views on motion and gravity. He did not try to *answer* the question 'Why does a body keep moving?' He simply stopped asking it! He said it was better for people 'to pronounce that wise, ingenious and modest sentence, "I know it not" rather than to suffer to escape from their mouths and pens all manner of extravagances'. Suppose it was just as 'natural' for a body to move as to stay still. Then ought we not rather to try to discover what *stops* moving objects? *What have you already seen to be in continuous motion (a) on the Earth and (b) elsewhere?* (18)

The 400th anniversary of Galileo's birth in Pisa was celebrated in 1964. His father followed an ancient practice of giving his first-born a Christian name which was a slight variation of his surname—Galileo Galilei. Galileo was first sent to a monastery and then to the University of Pisa to study medicine and philosophy. When he was 19 he noticed that a chandelier in Pisa Cathedral seemed to swing to and fro with the same period regardless of the amplitude of the swings. At this time he started taking a great interest in mathematics and soon decided to give up medicine to study mathematics. By the age of 22 he had invented a hydrostatic balance. Two years later he produced an essay on centres of gravity. Then he investigated the laws which govern the motions of solid bodies. His early work brought him such distinction that by the age of 25 he was appointed Professor of Mathematics at the University of Pisa.

We have already seen that, as Galileo had no way of measuring very short time intervals, he reduced the acceleration of a ball pulled down by gravity by allowing the ball to roll down an inclined plane. In this way he was able to use a water clock to measure the time taken and hence the acceleration of the ball. *Is the displacement of such a ball proportional to the time from rest?* (19) *Is its displacement proportional to its velocity?* (20)

It is doubtful whether Galileo ever actually calculated the acceleration of gravity for a freely falling body, although one record states that he measured the time taken for an iron ball to fall 300 feet. It took 5 seconds. *What value does this give for the acceleration of gravity?* (21) *What is the accepted value today expressed in ft/s^2?* (22)

We have also seen that the mass of a freely falling body does not affect its acceleration. *Why, then, does a lump of lead fall more quickly than a sheet of paper?* (23) *Under what conditions would they fall at the same rate?* (24)

Practical Puzzle 25. *If mass does not affect the rate of fall of a body, will the mass of a pendulum bob affect the time it takes to fall, in an arc, from a given height to the bottom of its swing? In other words will the mass of the bob affect the period of a pendulum?*

Think this out carefully and then test your conclusion by an experiment. What factors will you have to keep constant during the experiment?

Two inclined planes

Galileo placed two inclined planes together so that a ball would run down one and up the other. You can repeat his experiment with a piece of curtain rail.

Experiment 5.5. Bend a piece of curtain rail until it is similar to ABC in Fig. 82. Now roll a ball bearing down AB, and note where it starts and to what point it rises on BC. Does it rise to exactly the same height?

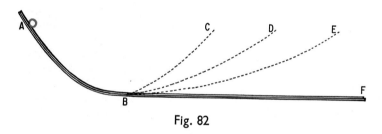

Fig. 82

Repeat this experiment with the rail bent to positions ABD, ABE and finally ABF (BF is horizontal).

Does the ball always rise to the same height? What about ABF?

When Galileo did this experiment with two inclined planes he discovered that the ball did not rise quite as high on the second plane. So he did a 'thought experiment'. He said in effect, 'Suppose this experiment could be repeated *without friction*. Then the ball would rise to exactly the same height every time'. He could not, of course, test this 'thought experiment' in practice, as it is impossible completely to get rid of all frictional forces. Here is another experiment he used to investigate the problem.

Experiment 5.6. Fix up a pendulum on a heavy retort stand as shown (Fig. 83) and release the bob from a height indicated by the metre stick. When it reaches the vertical position the thread will touch the clamp which should be rigidly fixed and the bob will rise steeply. Does it rise to the original height? Would it rise to the same height if the clamp were removed? Try it.

Galileo said that, but for friction, the ball on the inclined planes would also tend to reach its original height. This would be true for positions ABC, ABD and ABE (Fig. 82). If BF is horizontal the

Fig. 83

ball would never be able to reach its original height, and so it would go on and on for ever! If there is no friction then a moving body should go on moving, as there is nothing to stop it.

The Linear Air Track

In earlier experiments you reduced friction by using a balloon puck or polystyrene beads. *What was the result?* (26) *What happens if a block of ice or a heavy stone is pushed across a frozen pond?* (27) In the following experiments we will attempt to measure the velocity of bodies moving with little friction.

Demonstration 5.7. (a) A linear air track[10] may be constructed from a length of Dexion Speedframe (6 ft or more). Holes 3/64th inch in diameter are drilled at $\frac{1}{2}$ inch intervals along the top and sides. A vehicle about 4 in long can then be made from $\frac{1}{8}$ in perspex (Fig. 84). If given a push, it runs along the track on a

Fig. 84

cushion of air supplied by a vacuum cleaner. A drinking straw attached to the vehicle enables us to take stroboscopic photographs using high speed 35 mm film in an ordinary camera, but immediate results are possible using a Polaroid camera[11] and 3000 A.S.A. film. The track may be illuminated by a Xenon flasher[5.19]. Alternatively, a rotating disc[3] can be placed in front of the camera and two 100 watt bulbs used in reflectors.

Fig. 85

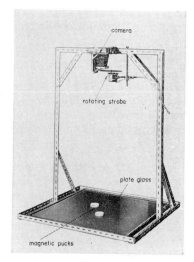

Fig. 86

Photograph a vehicle moving along an air track. Does its speed vary as it moves along? Fig. 38, page 21, shows a photograph of a vehicle moving along a horizontal linear air track.

(b) An alternative method of measuring the speed of the vehicle at two different points is illustrated in Fig. 85. Each electric stop clock[2,9] is switched photo-electrically[10] as a card attached to the vehicle interrupts a beam of light.

Demonstration 5.8. You can build a dry-ice puck as follows. Take a ring magnet from an old TV set (Mullard FD112) and glue a metal disc on one face. Put a piece of dry ice in the cavity thus formed and place the puck on a *level* sheet of plate glass. The lower face of the magnet must be absolutely smooth and clean. If the top of the puck is painted white and the under side of the plate glass is painted black, a strobe photograph can be taken as the puck moves along the glass. A rotating disc (Fig. 86) or a Xenon lamp (Fig. 87) may be used.

(Complete kits for this experiment are available commercially[3]. A CO_2 cylinder[3] is a convenient source of dry ice.)

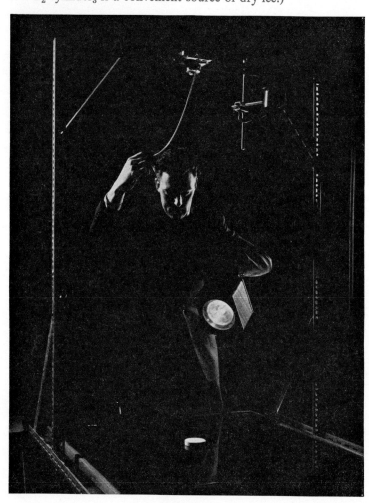

Fig. 87

From the Esso film "Experiments in Force and Motion"

Photograph a dry ice puck as it moves across the glass plate. Fig. 88 shows such a photograph. Is the puck moving at a constant speed? Is it moving in a straight line?

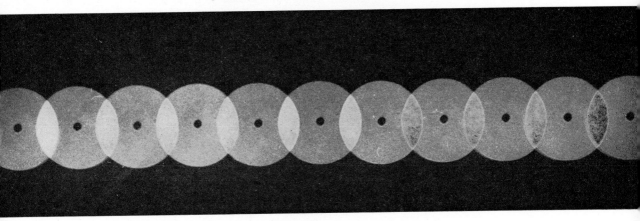

Fig. 88

The vehicle on the linear air track could move in only one dimension—along the track. Balanced forces acting on the sides prevented its turning to the left or right, and the weight of the vehicle was balanced by the force of the air pushing it up. The forces on the vehicle were therefore balanced.

Were there any sideways forces acting on the ice puck? (28) Was it free to move to the left or the right? (29) Was the weight of the puck balanced? (30) Were there any unbalanced forces acting on the puck? (31) In how many dimensions was the puck free to move? (32)

There is no experiment we can conduct in a school laboratory in which a body is free to move in three dimensions. To study such movement we would have to get rid of gravity, or balance its pull whilst the body rose or fell. Spacecraft once clear of the Earth's pull do however move very nearly in a straight line at constant speed. Fig. 89 shows the path taken by a space-ship on its flight to the moon. When no unbalanced force was acting on it the spacecraft 'went straight'! Electrons, in a cathode-ray tube, may also move very nearly in a straight line.

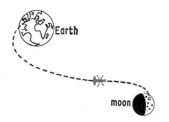

Fig. 89

This property of matter which keeps it still or travelling with a uniform velocity we call inertia. This does not explain it—it simply labels it. Galileo's answer to the ancient question, 'What keeps a stone moving?' was simply, 'We do not know, but we can discover what makes it slow down or stop'. The assertion that a stationary body stays that way and that a moving body goes on moving if there is no friction is sometimes called Galileo's *Law of Inertia*. Later Newton restated it in one of his Laws of Motion.

Projectiles

When you throw a stone horizontally its inertia (mass) tends to keep it moving horizontally but the pull of gravity (weight) tries to make it fall vertically. Galileo studied this type of motion and came to an important conclusion.

Experiment 5.9. (*a*) Throw one stone horizontally, and at the same instant drop another stone so that it falls vertically to the ground (Fig. 90). Which stone strikes the ground first? Is the vertical acceleration the same for both?

Fig. 90

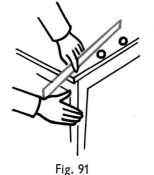

Fig. 91

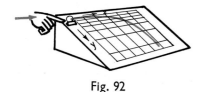

Fig. 92

(*b*) A metre stick can be used to project two golf balls at different speeds as shown in Fig. 91.

Project 5.10. Place a piece of carbon paper on top of a sheet of graph paper on a drawing board. Tilt the board and project a large steel ball horizontally as shown in Fig. 92. The path of the ball will be marked on the graph paper. Find the Y displacements which correspond to 1, 2, 3 . . . units of displacement in the X direction.

Project 5.11. Use a piece of apparatus which projects one sphere horizontally and at the same time releases another to fall vertically$_{3,12}$. Do the spheres strike the floor at the same time? What does this tell you?

The apparatus illustrated in Fig. 96 (page 56) was used to release a ball-bearing which was travelling (almost) horizontally at a constant speed. At the same instant a stationary ball-bearing was released from the same height. Fig. 93 shows a strobe photograph of the two spheres as they fall. *Does the projected sphere move at a constant rate in a horizontal direction?* (*33*) *Is the vertical motion the same in each case?* (*34*) *Can you describe the vertical motion?* (*35*) *Does the vertical motion of a body falling under gravity depend on its horizontal motion?* (*36*) *Does the horizontal motion depend on the vertical motion?* (*37*) The answers to these questions should help you to find Galileo's important conclusion.

Here are some experiments which demonstrate the same principle.

Demonstration 5.12. Use the apparatus illustrated in Book 1, Fig. 147 to project drops of water. If they are illuminated by a

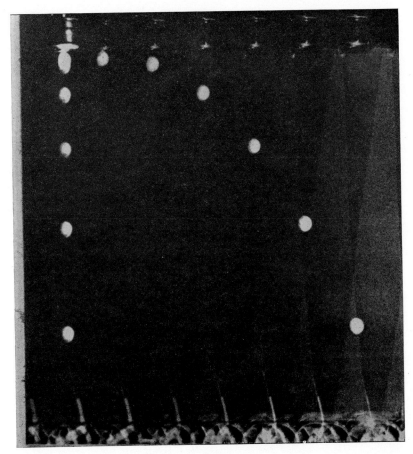

Fig. 93

strobe lamp or a rotating disc in front of a slide projector, an interesting effect is obtained. The water jet can also be interrupted by a ticker timer or an Advance vibration generator$_{13}$ coupled to the rubber tubing.

Demonstration 5.13. A gun is aimed at a monkey hanging on a tree. If the monkey lets go at the instant the gun is fired will the bullet hit him? Has the bullet fallen with the same acceleration as the monkey? Does it matter how fast the bullet is travelling? Does it matter what the mass of the bullet is?

To answer these questions fix up the apparatus illustrated in Fig. 94. A tin can represents the monkey, and the circuit is completed via a strip of aluminium foil glued round the cork. Try a 'bullet' of greater mass.

Project 5.14. Here is an experiment to try some day when you are in a bus or train travelling straight at a constant speed. Hold up a penny and release it. How does it fall? Can you explain how this motion confirms Galileo's Law of Inertia?

Problems

38. *Do you tend to fall forwards or backwards when you jump from a moving bus? Why?*

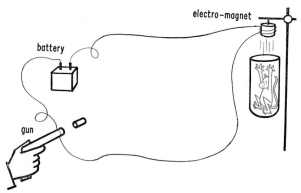

Fig. 94

39. *A ball is rolled across the floor of a railway carriage so that when the train is at rest the ball moves at an angle of 90° to the sides of the carriage. Draw a diagram showing its path, relative to the carriage, when the train is (a) moving with uniform velocity (b) accelerating and (c) decelerating.*

40. *A metal ball dropped from an aeroplane flying at 100 m/s reaches the ground after 20 seconds. Take g as 10 m/s² and ignore air resistance.*

(a) *What is the ball's horizontal speed just before it touches the ground?*

(b) *What is its vertical speed then?*

(c) *At what height was the plane flying when the ball was dropped?*

(d) *How far did the ball travel horizontally between release and impact?*

(e) *What was the average vertical speed of the ball?*

(f) *What was the average horizontal speed of the ball?*

(g) *What was the displacement of the ball from the moment it was dropped until it landed?*

(h) *What was the average velocity of the ball?*

Let Newton be!

> Nature and Nature Laws lay hid in night,
> God said, 'Let Newton be!' and all was light.
> (Alexander Pope)

In 1642 Galileo died. In the same year a child was born into the home of a Lincolnshire farmer called Newton. The child was christened Isaac. He was a sickly, shy boy and after four years at King's School, Grantham, where he made little progress, his mother took him away from school and decided to make him a farmer.

As a boy Isaac was fond of making mechanical toys. He built, for example, a wooden windmill and used a mouse to turn the sails! He also built waterclocks and sundials. This was good experience, as later he had to build much of his experimental apparatus himself. His uncle saw that Isaac was not really suited to farming, and eventually persuaded his mother to let him return to school.

One day Isaac was being pestered by the class bully, who kicked him in the stomach. Isaac, who could stand for this no longer, challenged the aggressor to a fight and proceeded to beat him up! This success seemed to give Isaac a new confidence in his physical and mental capabilities! He never looked back. From school he went to Trinity College, Cambridge.

Because of the plague in 1665 the University was closed and Newton returned home for two years of 'private study'. He spent those years reading, writing and *thinking*. It was in those two years of quiet, before he was 25 years old, that the foundations were laid for all his great discoveries. When he was 27 Newton was appointed Professor of Mathematics at Cambridge. He became so absorbed by his subject that he often forgot about things such as meals! Many amusing stories suggest that he became very absent-minded and unpractical about every-day things. He once cut a hole in the door of the house to allow the cat to come in and out. When the cat had kittens he cut a number of smaller holes—one for each kitten!

Newton's great genius lay in his ability to take the discoveries and theories of other men and fit them into a single, logical pattern. Professor A. N. Whitehead said that this 'has some right to be considered as the greatest single intellectual success which mankind has achieved'. Newton, however, recognised his indebtedness to other men. He once said, 'If I have seen further than other men it is because I have stood on the shoulders of giants'.

One of these giants was Galileo, and Newton's First Law of Motion owes its origin to him. If a piece of rock, say, is stationary, it will stay that way, but once on the move it will go on moving in a straight line forever if no unbalanced force acts on it. The idea that rocks (unlike humans!) want to 'go straight' all the time is difficult to imagine, because we cannot easily arrange a system in which no unbalanced (or resultant) force acts. *Can you give one practical example?* (41)

Perhaps the simplest way of stating Newton's First Law is as follows: 'A body stays at rest or moves with uniform velocity unless an unbalanced force acts on it.'

What does this law say about force? (42) *Is friction a force?* (43) *Why do motorists wear safety belts?* (44) *Why might a double decker bus topple if it were going round a sharp corner very quickly?* (45) *What steps are taken to reduce the likelihood of this happening?* (46)

Problem 47. A car is travelling at a constant velocity of 40 miles per hour (north) along a level road. Which of the following statements is correct? The unbalanced force acting on the car is (a) directed vertically up (b) directed vertically down (c) directed towards the south (d) directed towards the north (e) zero.

Satellite Motion

Newton once suggested a 'thought experiment'. He imagined a very high mountain from the top of which a bullet could be fired. The bullet might follow the path marked A. A faster bullet would follow path B. If it could be fired fast enough the bullet would circle the Earth as it fell so that it would return to its starting point. Newton had suggested the first artificial Earth satellite!

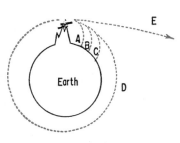

Fig. 95

As it circled the Earth the bullet could be moving at a constant speed. *Would an unbalanced force act on it?* (48) *Would it be accelerating towards the Earth?* (49) *Explain your answer.* (50)

Why is it essential to fire the bullet (or launch a satellite) from a point well above the Earth's surface; say 200 miles? (51)

If you were inside an orbiting satellite would you be 'weightless'? (52) *Does this mean that there would be no gravitational pull on you?* (53) *If you think there would be such a pull, how do you explain this apparent 'weightlessness'?* (54)

What would happen if the bullet could be fired at a very much higher velocity so that it took path E? (55)

Optional Extras

Project 5.15. Attach a piece of wood about 18 in high to a trolley as shown in Fig. 96. To the top of the wood fix a solenoid supplied by a 9 volt battery via a contact which can be broken by the movement of a light lever. Attach a heavy ball bearing to the solenoid, and then switch off so that the ball falls on to a plasticine mat on the trolley. Note where the ball falls.

Now allow the trolley to run at a constant speed along a friction-compensated runway. Fix a pin at the side of the runway so that it moves the lever as the trolley passes, thus breaking the circuit. Where does the ball fall now? Did the ball continue to move at the same horizontal speed as it fell? Does this confirm or disprove Galileo's Law of Inertia?

Problems

56. *Fig. 97 shows a strobe photograph of a ball released from a trolley. Was the trolley moving? Was the camera fixed to the bench or to the trolley? Taking g, the acceleration of gravity, as*

Fig. 96

Fig. 97

10 m/s² and the flash frequency as 25 per second, find approximately the time taken for the ball to fall (in seconds), the vertical distance through which the ball falls (in metres), and the speed of the trolley (in metres per second).

What can you say about the horizontal motion of the ball before and during its fall?

57. *Fig. 98 shows three photographs of the same event. Can you explain them stating where the camera was placed for each photograph?*

Fig. 98 (*b*)

Photo by Gordon Severn

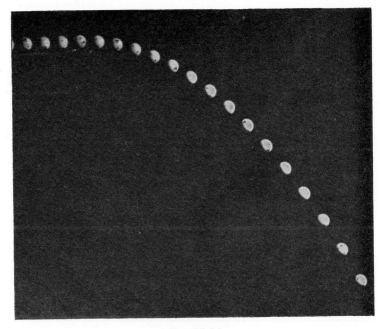

Fig. 98 (c)

Photo by Gordon Severn

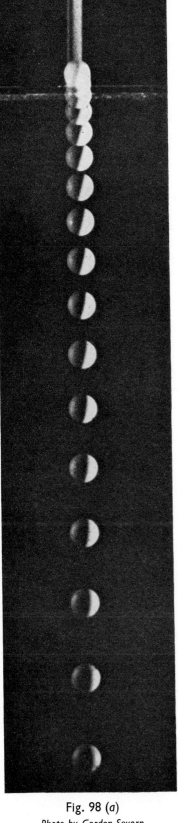

Fig. 98 (*a*)

Photo by Gordon Severn

Newton 2—How to Measure Force

CHAPTER 6

Force

Force was 'invented' to explain the fact that things do not move with constant velocities! This may not be how you would describe force; nevertheless it is, in effect, how Galileo and Newton regarded it. This does not mean that there are no forces acting on a body which is either moving at a constant velocity or is at rest. A train, for example, travelling at a steady 80 mi/h has many strong forces acting on it, and a rope used for a tug-of-war may be stationary yet subjected to strong forces.

Fig. 99

What kind of force, then, is necessary to change the motion of a body? Newton referred to a motive force, others have spoken of a driving force, a resultant force, an accelerating force, a net force, or an unbalanced force. All these names refer to the same thing. We will use the term *unbalanced force*. If 2,000 newtons is exerted by the left-hand side of the tug-of-war team and 2,100 newtons by the right-hand side, the rope and teams will move to the right. We speak of an unbalanced force of 100 newtons. It is this unbalanced force and not the total force with which we are concerned when we study motion.

If you deposit £30 in a bank during a year and during the same period you write out cheques for £50, you will end up with an overdraft ('unbalanced amount') of £20. It is this *unbalanced amount* which is likely to produce activity on the part of the bank manager!

No matter how large may be the forces which act on a body, it is only the *unbalanced force* which causes a change in the body's motion. In the following experiments we will study how the motion of a trolley is altered when a constant unbalanced force acts on it.

Experiment 6.1. For this and many other experiments you will require a set of trolleys$_6$, a vibrating timer$_{3,4}$ and a runway$_{3,10}$. A board about 5 ft × 1 ft, preferably covered with Formica and mounted on Dexion Speedframe, is ideal. A screw adjustment at one end allows the slope of the track to be altered readily.

Attach with Sellotape a metre length of ticker tape to the trolley. Arrange the apparatus as shown in Fig. 100 with the track sloping slightly. Start the timer and give the trolley a sharp push to start it moving down the track. Analyse the tape to see if the trolley

Fig. 100

moved along at a constant speed. If the trolley did not run down the track at a constant speed, alter the slope and repeat the above procedure until it does. How will you know when the speed is constant?

You have obtained a *friction-compensated track*. Is there an unbalanced force acting on the trolley as it runs down with constant speed?

Experiment 6.2. For this and other experiments you should use a length of fine elastic$_3$ stretched by a fixed amount as a unit of force. The elastic may be fitted with brass eyelets for ease of manipulation.

Attach one end of the elastic to a trolley on a friction-compensated track and pull the other end of the elastic until the eyelet is in line with the leading edge of the trolley (Fig. 101). Practise pulling the

Fig. 101

trolley down the track keeping the elastic stretched by the same amount all the time. You will have to do this several times until you are expert at it!

Could we obtain the same result by attaching the other eyelet to a dowel on the other end of the trolley so that it would pull itself? Explain.

When you are confident that you can do this really well attach a length of ticker tape to the trolley (Fig. 101), switch on the timer and pull the trolley down the track. Was there a constant unbalanced force applied to the trolley? Did the elastic exert the same force on you? Was *this* an unbalanced force? If not, what balanced it?

Cut the ticker tape into lengths each having a group of ten spaces, and construct a tape chart (graph) showing how the speed altered with time. What kind of motion was produced?

As the timer produces 50 dots every second what time interval is represented by 10 spaces? What is the *change* of speed of the trolley between one time interval and the next? Now express this change of speed in metres per second. Was this *change of speed* reasonably constant? Having found the change of speed every fifth of a second (expressed in metres per second per fifth of a second), can you find the change of speed per second (in metres per second²)? What is this change of speed per second called?

Why was a friction-compensated track used for this experiment?

A constant unbalanced force produces a constant acceleration. *From the results of previous experiments what does this tell you about the force which gravity exerts on a body as it falls near the Earth's surface?* (1)

Acceleration and Force

In the next experiment you investigate the acceleration of a trolley when different unbalanced forces act on it. Use two equal lengths of identical elastic, placed side by side, and stretched by equal amounts to produce two units of force. Similarly three and four lengths of elastic will produce three and four units of force respectively. A nail pushed into a small cork provides a suitable means of holding the loose ends of the elastic threads.

Don't pull the elastic threads too hard. An over-stretched elastic is as useless as a broken test-tube!

Fig. 102

Experiment 6.3. Repeat Experiment 6.2 using 2, 3 and then 4 elastic threads in parallel (Fig. 102) to accelerate the trolley down the track. Analyse the tapes directly or by making tape charts and thus calculate the acceleration of the trolley for 1, 2, 3 and then 4 units of force.

Construct a graph showing how the acceleration of a given mass (1 trolley) varies with the unbalanced force acting on it. What do you conclude? Complete the following table of results, trying to find a way of combining F and a so that the result is approximately the same each time. Does this agree with the conclusion you reached from your graph?

Force (F)	1	2	3	4
acceleration (a)				

Acceleration and Mass

In the last experiment you kept the mass constant and varied the unbalanced force. In the next experiment you should investigate any changes of acceleration produced by the *same* unbalanced force acting on *different* masses. By stacking identical trolleys on top of one another you can investigate the acceleration of 1, 2, 3 and then 4 units of mass.

Experiment 6.4. Use (say) two elastic threads in parallel to pull one trolley down a friction-compensated track. Analyse the tape and thus find the acceleration produced.

Now stack another trolley on top of the first and check that the slope is friction-compensated for two trolleys. The slope will

Fig. 103

almost certainly have to be altered. Why is this? Once you are certain that the slope is friction compensated for two trolleys, apply the same unbalanced force as before (2 elastic threads) and calculate the acceleration (Fig. 103).

Repeat this procedure with three and then four trolleys stacked on top of one another. It is essential to check the friction compensation of the slope each time.

When you have found the acceleration produced by a constant force acting on 1, 2, 3 and 4 units of mass, plot a graph showing how the acceleration varies with mass. Are they directly proportional? Now complete the following table and try to find a way of combining *m* and *a* which gives approximately the same result every time. How, then, are these two quantities related?

mass (*m*)	1	2	3	4
acceleration (*a*)				

From the last experiments you discovered that the acceleration (*a*) of a body depends on its mass (*m*) and on the unbalanced force (*F*) applied to it. This information enables us to define a unit of force. In honour of the man who first defined force in this way the unit has been named the *newton*. When 1 newton (1N) acts on a mass of 1 kilogram (1 kg) an acceleration of 1 metre per second per second (1 m/s²) is produced. Use the relationships you discovered from the last two experiments to complete the following:

			Force						Mass			Acceleration
An unbalanced force of			1 N	acting on a mass of					1 kg	produces an acceleration of		1 m/s²
,,	,,	,,	5 N	,,	,,	,,	,,	,,	1 kg	,,	,,	,, ,,
,,	,,	,,	F N	,,	,,	,,	,,	,,	1 kg	,,	,,	,, ,,
,,	,,	,,	F N	,,	,,	,,	,,	,,	30 kg	,,	,,	,, ,,
,,	,,	,,	F N	,,	,,	,,	,,	,,	m kg	,,	,,	,, ,,

If the acceleration of a body of mass *m* kilograms is $\dfrac{F}{m}$ metres per second per second when a force of *F* newtons acts on it, we can write

$$a = \frac{F}{m}$$

This is Newton's Second Law of Motion. It states, in effect, that the acceleration (*a*) of a body is proportional to the unbalanced force (*F*) and inversely proportional to the mass (*m*) of the body. We can rewrite this statement as follows.

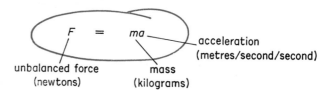

F = ma
unbalanced force (newtons)
mass (kilograms)
acceleration (metres/second/second)

Does this relationship agree with the results of your experiments?
(2) *If **m** is constant how are **a** and **F** related?* (3) *If **F** is constant how are **a** and **m** related?* (4)

Force is a vector quantity and, strictly speaking, its magnitude and direction should always be stated. You will find, however, that in many problems the direction of the forces, accelerations and velocities are not mentioned. In such cases you can safely assume that they refer to motion in one direction.

Practical Puzzles

5. *A trolley is pulled down a friction-compensated slope by 3 elastic threads in parallel. The acceleration is found to be 12 cm/s². The elastic threads are now tied end to end and pulled so that each is stretched by exactly the same amount as before (Fig. 104). What would be the acceleration of the trolley now?*

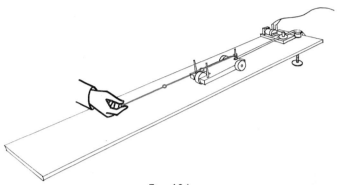

Fig. 104

6. *A card 20 cm long is attached to a trolley. The trolley is then allowed to run down a sloping track so that the card passes between a light source and a photo-transistor attached to a Panax scaler[8] or an electric stop-clock[2,9]. When the card interrupts the light falling on the transistor, the clock operates, thus measuring the time taken for the trolley to pass. The trolley takes 500 milliseconds to pass one point on the track. When started from the same point the trolley*

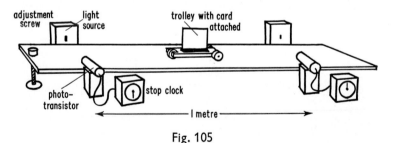

adjustment screw   light source   trolley with card attached

photo-transistor   stop clock

I metre

Fig. 105

takes 200 milliseconds to pass another point one metre further down the track. Find the speed at each of these points. Draw a rough graph showing the speed against time. What does the area below this graph represent? From the graph find the time taken for the trolley to travel the metre between the two points on the track. Find the acceleration of the trolley. How could you find the unbalanced force acting on the trolley?

7. *A trolley of mass 800 g is pulled down a friction compensated slope by an elastic thread. It travels 1 metre from rest in 4 seconds. Find the acceleration of the trolley and the force exerted by the elastic thread on it. If two trolleys were stacked on top of one*

another and pulled by 2 elastic threads in parallel, what would be the acceleration? What would be the acceleration if 3 trolleys were pulled by 3 threads and 4 trolleys by 4 threads?

Problems

8. *What unbalanced force is required to accelerate a mass of 0·8 kg from 25 cm/s to 125 cm/s in 5 seconds?*

9. *The speed of a 12 kg bicycle is reduced from 10 m/s to 5 m/s in 2·5 seconds. In what direction is the unbalanced force acting? What is its size?*

10. *If the displacement of a body is directly proportional to the time of motion from rest, what can you say about (a) the motion (b) the unbalanced force acting on it?*

11. *Why are the pistons in a car engine made of a light aluminium alloy?*

12. *If an unbalanced force always produces acceleration why can the speed of a car on a level road not be increased indefinitely?*

13. *A constant unbalanced force of 0·5 N was applied to a dry ice puck. The puck was then photographed stroboscopically at 10 flashes per second (Fig. 106). Find the acceleration of the puck and hence its mass.*

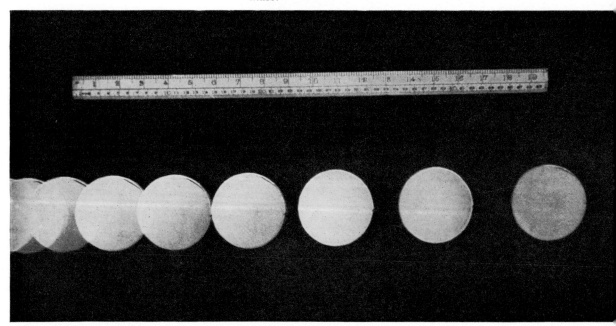

Fig. 106

14. *We can sometimes find the mass of atomic particles by observing the acceleration produced by a known magnetic or electric field acting on them.*

(a) An electron is accelerated at 10^{10} m/s² by an electric field. The force on the electron is 10^{-20} N. Find its mass.

(b) A proton of mass $1·66 \times 10^{-27}$ kg is moving horizontally with a constant velocity when it enters a vertical electric field. If the field exerts a force of 3×10^{-15} N on the proton, find the vertical acceleration of the proton. How would the field affect the horizontal velocity?

Gravity

Perhaps the best known of all the stories about Newton tells of the time when he was forced to leave Cambridge because of the plague and return to his home in Lincolnshire. As he watched an apple fall from a tree one day he wondered if the same force might not keep the moon circling the Earth. Whether or not such an incident really marked the beginning of Newton's theory of gravitation is not very important, but you might like to remember that the force exerted by gravity on an average-sized apple is approximately 1 newton!

I. Newton

Fig. 107

'g'

We have already found that, regardless of its mass, a body accelerates at 9·8 m/s² when falling freely under gravity. This acceleration is usually denoted by the italic letter 'g'. It is unfortunate that the same symbol, in Roman type, is now used for grams, but the context should enable you to distinguish them.

From the acceleration (g) we can calculate the force (in newtons) acting on a body. Suppose a mass of 1 kg is falling freely. Then from

$$F = ma = mg$$

we obtain

$$F = 1 \text{ kg} \times 9\text{·}8 \text{ m/s}^2$$
$$= 9\text{·}8 \text{ kg m/s}^2$$
$$= 9\text{·}8 \text{ newtons}$$

The force acting on a mass of 1 kg is therefore 9·8 newtons. This is sometimes referred to as 1 *kilogram force* (1 kgf).

What will be the gravitational force acting on 2 kg, 5 kg, m kg? (15) *Is the force (weight) directly proportional to the mass?* (16) The experimental fact that all bodies fall with the same acceleration (g) at any particular part of the Earth's surface, coupled with Newton's Second Law ($F = W = mg$), justifies our earlier assumption that we can use weight (W) as a measure of mass (m). At any given place they are *directly proportional*.

To avoid the difficulty of thinking of 'g' as an acceleration when a body is at rest (!) you may prefer to consider it as a measure of *gravitational field strength*. As $g = \dfrac{W}{m}$, we can express the gravitational field strength of the earth as 9·8 newtons per kilogram. This means that the force acting on every kilogram of mass at the Earth's surface (i.e. its weight) is 9·8 newtons.

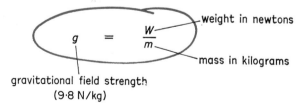

Of course if we are considering freely falling bodies we shall still think of 'g' as an acceleration of 9·8 m/s². Accurate measurements have shown that g varies between 9·78 m/s² at the equator and

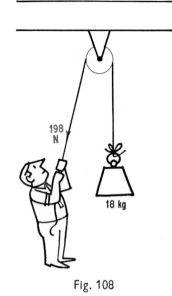

Fig. 108

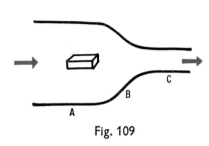

Fig. 109

9·83 m/s² at the poles. *Can you suggest a reason for this difference?* (17) *Would the period of a pendulum be greater at the equator than at the poles?* (18)

To save time you can take 'g' as 10 m/s² or 10 N/kg for all the problems in this book. *Roughly what is the percentage error involved using this approximation?* (19) *Can you show that the unit 'm/s²' is exactly the same as the unit 'N/kg'?* (20)

Problems

21. *A man exerts a force of 198 N on a rope attached to an 18 kg box (Fig. 108). Ignoring friction and the weight of the rope, find the acceleration of the box. How much work is done by the man in raising the box 5 metres? Where has the energy gone?*

22. (*a*) *If a rocket rises vertically from the Earth with a constant thrust, three things are likely to affect its acceleration. Can you say what they are and how they will alter the rocket's acceleration?*

(*b*) *Before blast-off, a mass hanging on a spring in a rocket stretches the spring by 10 cm. As the rocket rises vertically the spring stretches by a further 30 cm. Find the acceleration of the rocket. What is the thrust produced by the rocket motors if the mass of the rocket is 10^4 kg?*

23. *Water flowing at a constant speed through a wide tube (A) carries a rectangular block which moves at the same speed as the water (Fig. 109). How will the speed of the block when it reaches section C compare with its speed in section A? What happens to the block at B? What does this tell you about the forces exerted on the back and the front of the block at B? How does the fluid pressure at A compare with that at C? Would an unbalanced force act on the block at A, B and C?*

24. *A horizontal force of 3 N acts on a 10 kg block of dry ice lying on a sheet of glass. Assuming that there is no friction, what will be the acceleration of this block? How far will it travel from rest in 2 seconds?*

Vectors

A force has magnitude and direction and can be represented by a vector. In Fig. 23 (chap. 2) the two vectors were added by joining them together tail to tip. The resultant was obtained by joining the tail of one to the tip of the other. Note that the *tail* of the resultant is joined to a *tail* and the *tip* of the resultant is joined to a *tip*. In the next experiment you should test whether or not this kind of vector addition can be applied to forces.

Experiment 6.5. Attach a strong elastic band to a board at A (Fig. 110) and pull the other end with two spring balances. Place a sheet of paper under the balances and mark points O, B and C. Note the readings on the balances (X and Y newtons).

Measure the angle BOC and construct a vector diagram of the two forces (Fig. 111). Remove one of the spring balances and pull the remaining balance until the end of the elastic band is again over point O. As this single spring balance is now stretching the elastic band in exactly the same way as were the two balances

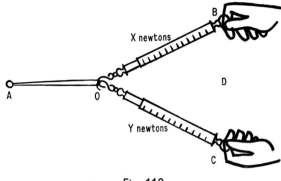

Fig. 110

before, we can say that this single force exerted by the balance is equivalent to the original two forces. This force is therefore the *resultant* of these forces.

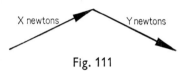

Fig. 111

Mark on the paper the point D to indicate the direction of the resultant and note the reading on the balance (R newtons). This is the magnitude of the resultant. How does this resultant compare with that obtained from Fig. 111 using the vector rule?

When two spring balances were attached to the rubber band in the above experiment how many forces were acting at O (25) Were the forces balanced? (26) Such a system is said to be in *equilibrium.*

The force exerted by the elastic band keeps the other two forces (X and Y) in equilibrium (Fig. 112). It is therefore called the

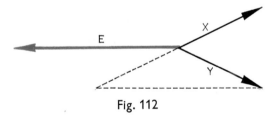

Fig. 112

equilibrant (E). How does the equilibrant (E) compare with the resultant (R)? (27) *If you draw a vector triangle for the three forces X, Y and E how do the arrows point?* (28)

You can see, then, that when three forces acting at a point (O in the above case) are in equilibrium, their vectors form a closed triangle with the arrows pointing in sequence round it. This statement is sometimes referred to as the 'triangle of forces'.

In the following experiment you can produce a triangle of forces for three forces in equilibrium.

Experiment 6.6. For this experiment you will require a circular disc of hardboard about 14 inches in diameter, 3 Terry clips (No. 80/00), each with a 1 inch nail soldered to it (Fig. 113), a small split ring, and a number of long identical elastic bands.

Attach 3 elastic bands to the split ring. Fix the clips to the edge of the hardboard disc and loop one elastic band over each nail as shown. Adjust the positions of the clips until the split ring is in

Fig. 113

the centre of the disc. This can be done more easily if a white spot, about the size of the split ring, is painted in the centre of the disc. What can you say about the length of each elastic band now? What about the force each exerts?

Place a sheet of paper under the elastic bands and mark their directions. Do the 3 forces pass through one point? Draw a vector diagram. Is it a closed triangle?

Repeat the above experiment using other groups of elastic bands to produce forces of 1, 2, 2 or 1, 2, 4 or 2, 3, 4 units. Construct vector diagrams for the forces produced.

Can you find a way to add together 4 forces acting at a point; for example forces of 1, 2, 3 and 4 units?

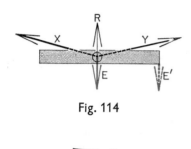

Fig. 114

Fig. 115

If three forces X, Y and E (Fig. 114) keep a body in equilibrium, the forces can be represented by a triangle of forces (Fig. 115). The forces act through one point O, and the resultant of X and Y is R (equal in magnitude and opposite in direction to E). *If the force E were moved right to E' and the sizes of the forces remained the same as before, could the same triangle of forces represent the three forces acting on the body? (29) Would the body be in equilibrium? (30) If not, how would it move? (31) Under what circumstances does the 'triangle of forces' represent three forces* in equilibrium? (32) *What conditions must be fulfilled for three forces to be in equilibrium? (33)*

Problems

34. *A dry ice puck of mass 500 g is pulled by 2 elastic threads each exerting a horizontal force of 0·1 N. Find the acceleration of the puck when the angle between the threads is (i) 0°, (ii) 30°, (iii) 60°, (iv) 90° and (v) 120°.*

Fig. 116

35. *A tractor is stuck in a ditch and so the driver ties a rope to the tractor and then to a tree 10 metres from it (Fig. 116). He then pushes with a force of 300 newtons at right angles to the centre of the rope. What force is being exerted on the tractor when the driver has displaced the centre of the rope by 0·5 metres? Neglect the small stretch in the rope.*

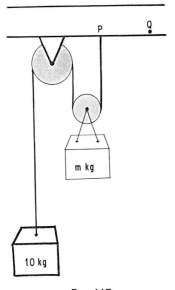

Fig. 117

36. *A pulley system is arranged as shown in Fig. 117. Assuming the rope to be weightless and the pulley to be friction free, find the combined mass of the movable pulley and the mass m, if the system is in equilibrium. If now the rope is removed from point P and moved along to Q, what will happen to the two masses? Explain your answer.*

37. *Fig. 118 and Fig. 119 show the path of a ball projected horizontally. Can you explain its horizontal motion (red dots) in terms of Newton's First Law of Motion, and its vertical motion (black dots) in terms of Newton's Second Law?*

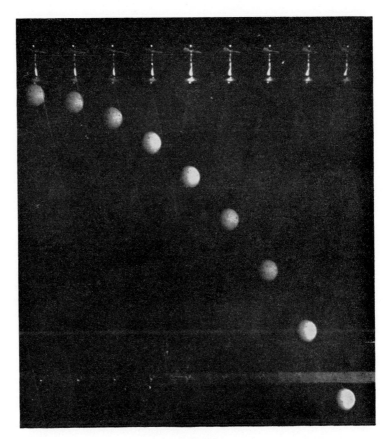

Fig. 118

38. *A 50g stone is placed in a catapult. The stone is released horizontally when the tension in each elastic is 30 newtons, and the angle between them is 20°. What force acts on the stone? What is the initial acceleration of the stone? Ignoring air friction, what can you say about the vertical and the horizontal motions of the stone when it leaves the catapult? Sketch the path of the stone.*

39. *A monkey, weighing 50N hangs by its tail and one arm. If the angle between its arm and tail is 70° and the angle between its arm and the vertical 25°, find the tension in its tail.*

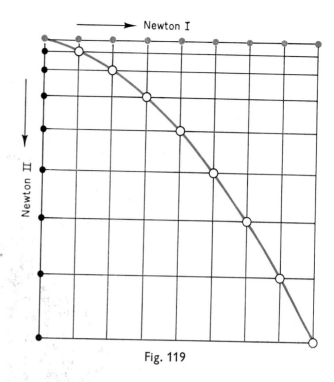

Fig. 119

Optional Extras

Everything is Squashy

There is no such thing as a perfectly rigid body. Even a fly landing on a steel beam deforms it to some extent. *Would you prefer to jump from a wall 3 metres high into sand or on to a concrete pavement?* (40) *Would you keep your legs straight or bend your knees?* (41) To stop your movement a force must be exerted on you. This may be a large force acting for a short time (as with the concrete) or a smaller force acting for a longer time (as in the case of the sand). On landing you would be travelling at about 8 m/s (from $v^2 = 2\ ad$). If it were possible to keep your knees straight and to land on the concrete so that the total deformation (of the concrete, your shoes and you) was only about 1 cm, you would have to come to rest from 8 m/s in that distance. Assuming the retardation to be constant throughout that centimetre, you can calculate your deceleration using $v^2 = 2\ ad$ again. This gives a deceleration of 3000 m/s², which is 300 g! Assuming your mass to be about 50 kg, the concrete would exert a force ($F = ma$) on you of 50 × 3000 = 150,000 newtons (about 15 tons force)! *What force would you exert on the concrete during that short time?* (42) *For how long would that force be acting?* (43)

If, on the other hand, you were to land on sand and sink, say, 20 cm into it, and if you bent your knees so that your body was gradually lowered another 60 cm, your deceleration would be 40 m/s² or 4 g. This corresponds to a force of 2000 newtons (about one-fifth of a ton force), which you could withstand without breaking any bones! *Assuming your deceleration was constant, how long would it last?* (44)

Problems

45. *A boy of mass 50 kg jumps in the air and lands with a speed of 4 m/s. If he bends his knees he comes to rest in 1 second (Δt). Find his deceleration. What is the average force (F) acting on him? If he had bent his knees only very slightly, he might have come to rest in 0·1 seconds (Δt). Find the deceleration and force (F) now. Finally find the deceleration and force (F) acting if he had kept his legs straight and come to rest in 0·01 seconds (Δt). Complete the following table.*

F			
Δt	1	0·1	0·01

Can you discover a way of combining F and Δt so that the result is the same each time? This is such an important quantity that we give it a special name—impulse.

46. *A fly, flying horizontally, bumps into a fast moving train coming in the opposite direction. The fly is stopped and its direction reversed. At one instant the fly must be stationary with respect to the Earth. At that instant it is in contact with the front of the train, so that the train must also be stationary with respect to the Earth. The fly has stopped the train. Do you agree? If not, why not?*

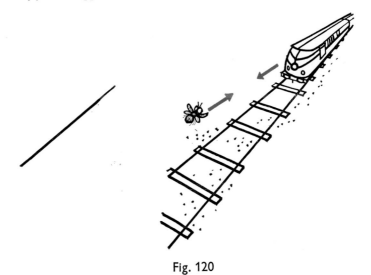

Fig. 120

47. *A 500 g football reaches 15 m/s by being in contact with a player's boot for 0·02 seconds. What was the average force exerted on the ball? What is the impulse (i.e. $F \times \Delta t$)?*

48. *How long will it take a force of 10 N to stop a mass of 2·5 kg which is moving at 20 m/s?*

49. *If a 1000 kg car accelerates at 2 m/s², what is the average force acting on it? If, after accelerating for 10 seconds, it crashes*

Fig. 121

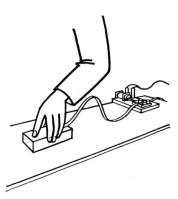

Fig. 122

into a wall and comes to rest in 0·5 seconds, find the average force of resistance and the impulse.

Practical Puzzles

50. *A salmon is tied to a spring balance by a string. When held stationary the balance reads 60 N. Find the mass of the salmon. What forces are acting on the salmon? Is there an unbalanced force acting on it? If the spring balance is jerked upwards (accelerated) what happens to the reading? If, later, the reading is 30 N can you explain what is happening? (Half the salmon has not been removed!) State the magnitude and direction of the salmon's acceleration.*

If the string were cut would an unbalanced force act on the salmon? If the fisherman were to jump down off a table whilst holding the spring balance with the salmon attached, what would the balance read whilst he was in the air?

If the salmon were weighed by a spring balance attached to the roof of a lift, what would happen to the reading when the lift was

(a) *ascending at a constant speed?*

(b) *descending at a constant speed?*

(c) *slowing down on its way up?*

(d) *slowing down on its way down?*

(e) *speeding up on its way up?*

(f) *speeding up on its way down?*

If the salmon were being weighed on a beam or a Butchart balance fitted to the floor of the lift, how would the results obtained during the above six motions compare with the results obtained when the lift was at rest?

51. *A piece of ticker tape is attached to a 2 kg block of wood or metal (Fig. 122). The tape is passed through a vibrating timer and the block given a sharp push along a horizontal bench. If the distances gone by the block every 1/10th second are 40, 36, 32, 28 and 24 centimetres, find the unbalanced force acting on the block. What is this unbalanced force due to?*

52. *Place a book on a table and lay a penny on it. Now move the book backwards and forwards several times, moving it very quickly in one direction and very slowly in the other. Can you explain the motion of the penny?*

53. *A 2 kg block is pulled along a horizontal bench by a spring balance reading 12 N. A ticker tape is attached to the block and 50 dots per second are recorded on the tape. If successive groups of 10 spaces between dots measure 10, 15, 20, 25 and 30 cm, find (a) the acceleration of the block (b) the unbalanced force acting on the block and (c) the frictional force acting on the block.*

54. *A string is attached to the trolley used in Project 5.15, page 56, and the other end after passing over a pulley is tied to a metal block (Fig. 123). As the trolley moves along a friction-compensated bench, the ball-bearing is released and strikes the plasticine 10 cm from the mark vertically below the electro-magnet. If the ball falls 45 cm vertically, what is the acceleration of the trolley? If the trolley and fittings have a mass of 1·8 kg, find the tension in the string. If the metal block has a mass of m kg, the gravitational force will be 10 m newtons. Is this the only force acting on the block?*

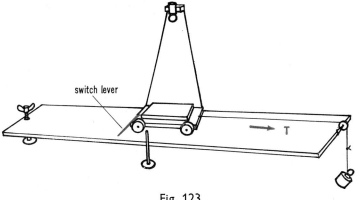

Fig. 123

The unbalanced force acting on the block will therefore be (10 m—tension) newtons. This is the force which causes the block to accelerate. As the block must accelerate at the same rate as the trolley you can find the mass of the block by solving

$$10\ m - tension = ma$$

i.e. $$W\quad -\quad T\quad = ma$$

Problems

55. *Two trolleys of mass 10 kg and 30 kg are placed on friction-compensated slopes as shown in Fig. 124. They are attached to a mass of m kg by threads containing spring balances. When released the mass drops 1 metre in 2 seconds. If the mass of the strings and balances can be neglected, find the acceleration of the trolleys and the readings on all three balances as the mass is dropping. What is the upward force acting on the mass? What is the downward force acting on the mass? What is the unbalanced force acting on the mass? It is this unbalanced force which causes the mass to accelerate. Using Newton's Second Law find the value of m.*

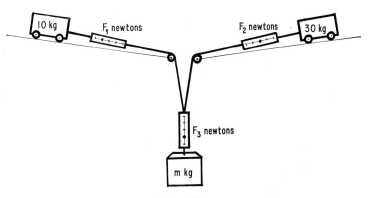

Fig. 124

56. *An unbalanced force of 10 N gives a mass of x kg an acceleration of 10 m/s². It also produces an acceleration of 20 m/s² when applied to a mass of y kg. If x and y are joined together, what acceleration would be produced by the same force?*

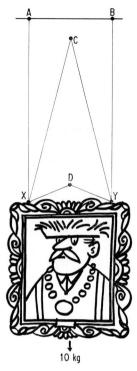

Fig. 125

57. *A yacht of the mass 1000 kg is driven west by a wind exerting 1000 N on it. The frictional resistance is 400 N east. Find the acceleration of the yacht and its velocity after 30 seconds from rest.*

58. *A space capsule is travelling at 10,000 m/s. If one stern rocket is turned on for 10 seconds the speed of the capsule increases by 20 m/s. Find how fast the capsule will be travelling if 3 such rockets operate for 1 minute. How long would it take to stop the capsule if the stern rockets were turned off and 6 retro-rockets used to slow it down? Assume that the thrust of each retro-rocket and stern rocket is the same.*

59. *If the mass of a body (m) and the unbalanced force (F) acting on it are both doubled, trebled, quadrupled, . . . what happens to the acceleration? Can you give an example of this kind of motion?*

60. *A picture of mass 10 kg can be suspended in 3 different ways (Fig. 125). If $CX = CY = 1$ metre and $XY = 50$ cm find the tension in the string. If $DX = DY = 26$ cm find the tension in the string. What is the tension in AX and BY? How will the lengths of AX and BY affect the tensions in them?*

61. *A shirt on a hanger at the centre of a 20-metre clothes line exerts a force of 2 newtons on it. If the line sags by 10 cm, find the tension in it. What would be the tension required to prevent the line from sagging?*

Visual Aids

8 mm Cassettes: Velocity and Acceleration in Free Fall[18] 80-256.
16 mm Films: What is Uniform Motion[23]? 21.7455.
Inertia (P.S.S.C.)[26] 2D.2641.
Inertial mass (P.S.S.C.)[26] 2D.2650.
Forces[23] 21.7453.
Forces (P.S.S.C.)[26] 2D.2572.
Force and Motion[28] (for teachers).

Newton 3—Conservation of Momentum

CHAPTER 7

Changelessness

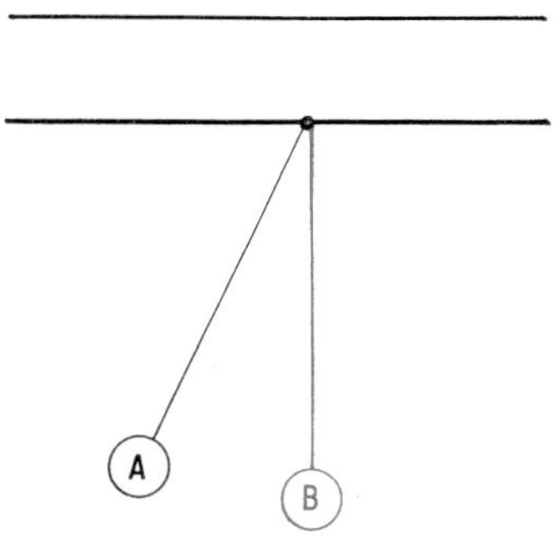

When the bob of a pendulum is at its highest point (A in Fig. 126) all its energy is *potential energy*. *What kind of energy has it as it passes through position B, where the potential energy has 'disappeared'?* (1) After swinging to the right the bob returns to position A where it again has potential energy. In this case energy is continually changing from one form (energy of position) to another (energy of movement), yet the total energy remains the same. It is true, of course, that if we leave the pendulum for a long time it will come to rest. Its energy would then have been changed into yet another form. *Can you suggest what this might be?* (2)

By investigating energy changes of all kinds scientists have come to believe that the total amount of energy in a system never changes although the form it takes does change. *List some of the types of energy change you have already encountered.* (3)

When scientists speak about the *conservation of energy* they mean that energy never appears from nowhere and never really disappears, although the form it takes alters.

Physicists are always on the look out for something that is conserved. The stretch of a coil spring divided by the force applied is constant (under certain conditions). *Whose law is this?* (4) The voltage applied to a simple circuit divided by the current flowing is also constant (under certain conditions). *What is this constant called?* (5)

Practically every physical law could be restated in such a way that some quantity was said to be conserved. When we find such a quantity we can predict how things will behave. Without changelessness (conservation), science and perhaps life itself would be impossible. Imagine trying to play cricket with a ball whose mass changed from minute to minute, or to ride a bicycle which was sometimes half and sometimes double your own mass. You need not worry—accurate experiments have shown that even during chemical reactions no change of mass can be detected. In 1908 Landott was unable to detect a change of 1 part in ten million.

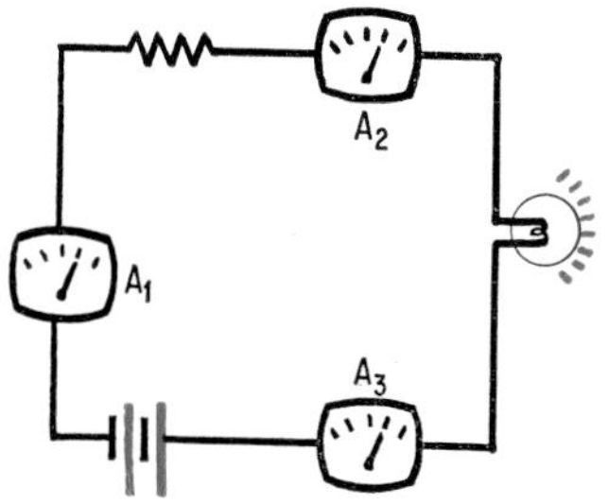

Experiments with series circuits (Fig. 127) have shown that electric charge flows at the same rate in every part of the circuit. Experiments in electrostatics were explained by assuming that the charge on one body could be shared with another body without loss provided both were insulated.

Although the so-called conservation laws, such as the conservation of energy, the conservation of mass and the conservation of charge, can never be *proved* to be correct, they are useful hypotheses which enable us to make predictions. Until they have been disproved we will accept them happily.

Fig. 126

Fig. 127

Motion

Does a car travelling at 110 mi/h have more or less motion than it does at 10 mi/h? Does a scooter travelling at 40 mi/h have the same amount of motion as a train travelling at that speed? As we haven't defined 'motion' these are difficult questions to answer. Nevertheless they should at least suggest factors to be considered when attempting to 'measure motion'. In the following experiment you are asked to look for some quantity that stays the same. Can you find anything which is conserved in motion?

Experiment 7.1. Fit a needle to one trolley$_6$ and a cork to a second trolley of equal mass (Fig. 128). Attach one end of a length of ticker tape to the first trolley and pass the other end of the tape through a ticker timer. Place the second trolley at the middle of a friction-compensated slope and start the ticker timer. Give the first trolley a sharp push so that it runs down the track at a constant speed. When the trolleys collide the needle is embedded in the cork, and the trolleys move off together. From the tape find the velocities of the trolleys before and after the collision.

Repeat this experiment with another trolley stacked on top of the stationary one (Fig. 129) so that you have one unit of mass moving before and three units of mass moving after the collision. Finally use three stacked trolleys so that you have one unit of mass before and four after the collision.

Mass before collision m_1	Velocity before collision v_1	?	Mass after collision m_2	Velocity after collision v_2	?
1			2		
1			3		
1			4		

Can you complete columns 3 and 6 in such a way that the quantity produced is conserved? Possible combinations of m and v might include $m + v$, $m - v$, $m \times v$, $\dfrac{m}{v}$, m^2v, $\dfrac{m^2}{v}$, $\dfrac{m}{v^2}$, etc., etc. The quantity you have found is so important that we give it a special name: *momentum*.

If you drop a lump of plasticine on the floor it does not bounce: it simply sticks to the floor. The plasticine and the Earth have collided inelastically. When two objects collide and stick together like this we have a *completely inelastic collision*. If, on the other hand, a ball is dropped on the floor so that it bounces back to its original height, we have a *completely elastic collision*.

In practice most collisions fall somewhere between these two extreme examples. For simplicity we first considered trolleys colliding inelastically, and we will now use trolleys fitted with elastic bands to investigate collisions which are very nearly completely elastic.

Fig. 128

Fig. 129

From the Esso film "Momentum and Collision Processes"

Experiment 7.2. Fix an aluminium nose, tape bracket, and length of ticker tape to a trolley. Fix another tape bracket tape and an elastic band to a second trolley as shown in Fig. 130. The tapes should run through the same ticker timer. Use two carbon discs back to back and pass one tape above the upper and the other below the lower disc.

Fig. 130

Place the second trolley at the middle of a friction-compensated track, start the ticker timer and push the first trolley down the track to collide elastically with the other. Analyse the tapes and find the velocity of each trolley before and after impact.

Repeat this experiment, allowing two stacked trolleys to run into one trolley. Finally let three stacked trolleys collide with a single trolley. Record your results.

Before impact

Mass of left hand body (m_1)	Velocity of left hand body (v)	Momentum before impact $(m_1 v)$ $\longrightarrow$
1		
2		
3		

After impact

Mass of left hand body (m_1)	Velocity of left hand body (v_1)	Momentum of left hand body $(m_1 v_1)$ $\longrightarrow$	Mass of right hand body (m_2)	Velocity of right hand body (v_2)	Momentum of right hand body $(m_2 v_2)$ $\longrightarrow$	Total Momentum $(m_1 v_1 + m_2 v_2)$ $\longrightarrow$
1			1			
2			1			
3			1			

From your results what can you say about the total momentum before and after each collision?

Explosion

In the following experiment you can investigate an explosion. Before the explosion the trolleys are at rest, so there is no momentum. You should calculate the total momentum after each explosion.

Experiment 7.3. For this experiment you will require a trolley with a spring-loaded plunger. When this is released it strikes another trolley so that the trolleys are propelled in opposite directions. To find their velocities attach two tapes to the trolleys as shown in

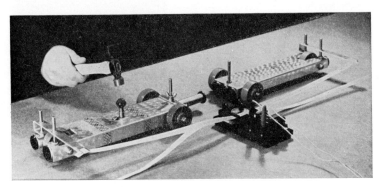

Fig. 131

Fig. 131, and pass the tapes through a ticker timer fitted with two carbon discs. Use mass ratios of 1:1, 1:2 and 1:3 by stacking trolleys and find the velocities and hence the total momentum each time. What do you conclude? Is momentum a vector quantity?

Mass of left hand trolley m_1	Velocity of left hand trolley v_1	m_1v_1 ←	Mass of right hand trolley m_2	Velocity of right hand trolley v_2	m_2v_2 →
1			1		
1			2		
1			3		

Problem 6. If a radio-active atom shot out a high-speed electron from its nucleus, would the remainder of the nucleus recoil with the same velocity? Would it have more or less momentum than the electron?

Practical Puzzles

7. *A trolley of mass 1 kg is attached to a ticker timer. It is given a push and, as it passes under mass m, the mass is released and lands*

on the trolley (*Fig. 132*). *Analysis of the tape shows that the average separation of the dots is 2 cm before the mass is dropped and 0·8 cm afterwards. If the ticker timer vibrates 50 times a second find the mass m. Can you suggest sources of error in this experiment?*

Fig. 132

8. *A ball bearing rolls down a curtain rail and strikes an identical ball at rest on the horizontal part of the rail (Fig. 133). Explain what happens. Is the collision elastic?*

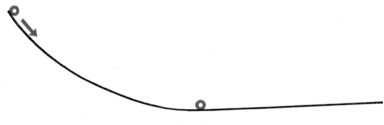

Fig. 133

9. (*a*) *Fig. 134 shows an inelastic collision between a moving and a stationary vehicle on a linear air track. Assuming that each vehicle had the same mass (0·2 kg) and that 1 cm on the photograph represents a velocity of 1 m/s, calculate the momentum before and after the collision. Are the vehicles moving from left to right or right to left in the photograph?*

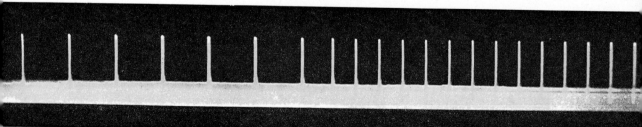

Fig. 134

(b) *If Fig. 135 represents an elastic collision between a moving and a stationary vehicle of mass 0·2 kg, find the momentum before and after the collision.*

Fig. 135

Collision—general case

So far we have considered only special types of impact, such as completely elastic and completely inelastic collisions. Can we measure momentum in a collision in which bodies are moving at different speeds in opposite directions before and after the collision? Is momentum (mass × velocity) conserved in such a case? To answer this question we will again use the linear air track.[10]

Demonstration 7.4. Vehicles of 1 and 2 units of mass are joined to form 3 units of mass on the right, and a vehicle of 2 units of mass is used on the left (Fig. 136). Drinking straws are used as before and a hinged shutter is fitted in front of the track. In Fig. 136 the shutter is shown in the 'down' position so that the top half of each drinking straw is visible to the camera. When the shutter is turned 'up' only the lower half of each straw is visible. At the instant when the two vehicles collide the shutter is switched. This enables a picture to be taken which shows the velocity of each vehicle before and after the collision.

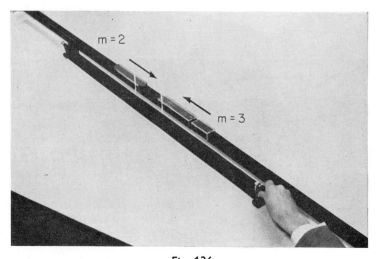

Fig. 136

Fig. 137 shows a photograph obtained from this experiment. Assuming the right-hand vehicle to have a combined mass of 0·3 kg, the left-hand vehicle to have a mass of 0·2 kg and taking 1 cm on the photograph to represent 1 m/s, find the total momentum (in magnitude and direction) before and after the impact.

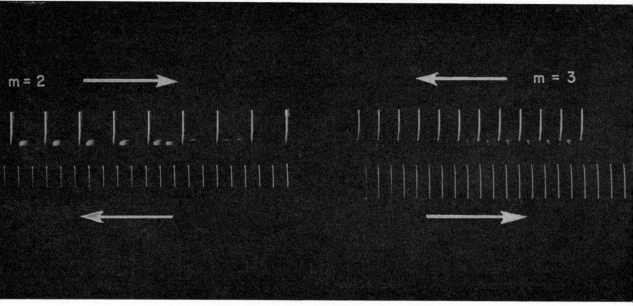

Fig. 137

Demonstration 7.5. (a) Can you suggest how your teacher could use the apparatus illustrated in Fig. 138 to find the velocity of an air pistol pellet?

Fig. 138

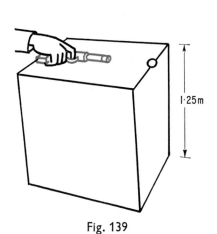

Fig. 139

(b) Can you think how the answer obtained in (a) could be checked, using a plasticine ball perched on the edge of a box? (Fig. 139).

(c) Finally both the above results can be checked using a scaler as an electric stop clock. Fire a pellet through two sheets of cardboard and then cover each hole with a $\frac{1}{8}$ in strip of thin silver paper (Fig. 140). When the next pellet breaks the first circuit the scaler is started, and when it breaks the second the scaler is stopped. How would you find the speed of the pellet with this apparatus?

(The last experiment is more easily conducted with an air rifle₃ than an air pistol.)

What happens to the momentum of a bullet fired into a tree? (10) *Can you suggest why, when investigating momentum, we used apparatus in which the frictional forces were very small?* (11)

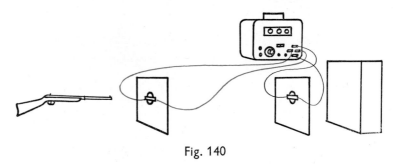

Fig. 140

Collision in two dimensions

One of the most fascinating applications of the conservation of momentum is the interpretation of the tracks of particles colliding elastically in a cloud or bubble chamber. In the following demonstration you can study an elastic collision between two magnets floating on a cushion of carbon dioxide. So far we have examined collisions between bodies free to move in only one dimension. The bodies have made physical 'contact' with each other. Now we look at bodies free to move in two dimensions and we see a collision in which these two bodies never touch!

Demonstration 7.6. Use the apparatus described in Demonstration 5.8 and *two* magnetic dry ice pucks of equal mass.

Place one puck in the middle of the plate and project the second towards it. They will collide elastically to produce the kind of picture shown in Fig. 141.

Can you think of a way of analysing the photograph to see if momentum was conserved in the original direction? Remember that momentum is a vector quantity.

Now measure the momentum of each puck, at right angles to the original direction. What do you discover? Do you notice anything about the angle formed?

Compare Fig. 141 and Fig. 142. The latter shows a collision between an alpha particle and the nucleus of a helium atom.

Project 7.7. The last experiment illustrated a magnetic collision. Can you suggest a method of producing an electric collision using a Van de Graaff generator, a table tennis ball coated with Aquadag₁₂ and a length of nylon thread?

What—no contact?

Although magnetic and electric collisions are obviously not produced by bodies in contact, it is not so easy to appreciate that all collisions are in a sense due to action-at-a-distance forces. When the atoms of one body come very close to those of another body they *repel* each other very strongly but they never really come into direct contact. The short-range atomic forces acting in such 'contact collisions' are electric forces.

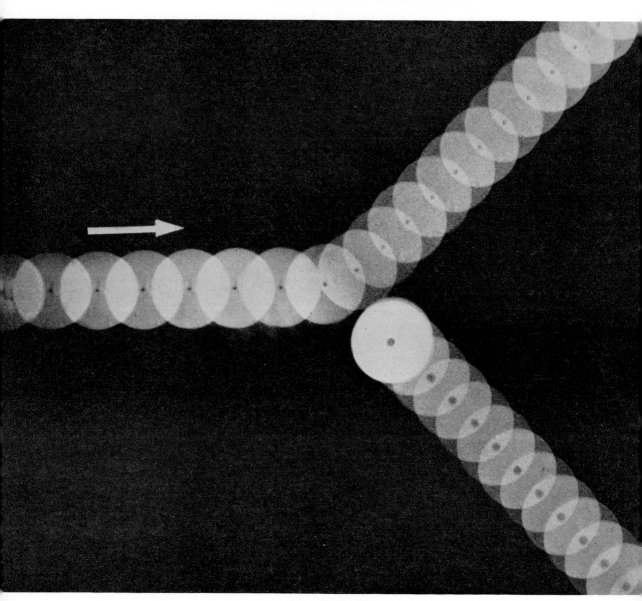

Fig. 141

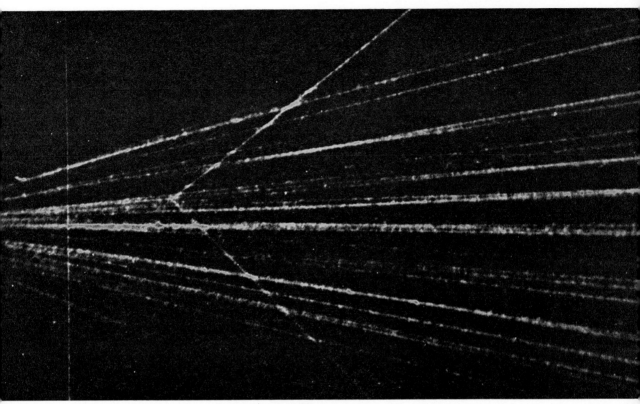

Fig. 142

By courtesy of Professor P. M. S. Blackett, F.R.S., Imperial College, London

Practical Puzzles

12. *A length of elastic connects two sets of trolleys as shown in Fig. 143. If all the trolleys are of equal mass and the original separation is 1 metre, where will they meet if both sets are released at the same instant? Justify your answer using the conservation of momentum.*

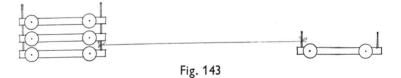

Fig. 143

13. *If Jack starts to run along a stationary trolley (Fig. 144) and then jumps off, what will happen to the trolley? Suppose Jill, who has the same mass as Jack, is running towards the trolley at the same*

Fig. 144

speed as Jack left it. Soon after Jack jumps off, Jill jumps on to and stays on the trolley. What will happen? Why?

Problems on Momentum

14. A squib is thrown into the air. When it reaches its maximum height it explodes in two pieces—one large, one small. Immediately after the explosion which piece will have (a) the greater velocity and (b) the greater momentum?

15. A 60 gram bullet fired from a 5 kg gun leaves with a speed of 600 m/s. Find the recoil speed.

16. If a 1 kg ball travelling south at 7 m/s collides with a 2 kg ball travelling in the same direction at 3 m/s, the velocity of the latter is increased to 4·5 m/s south. What happens to the 1 kg ball?

17. A Mini of mass 600 kg is involved in a head-on collision with a lorry of mass 3000 kg travelling at 15 m/s. The Mini is thrown on to the bonnet of the lorry which continues after the impact at 5 m/s in its original direction. How fast was the Mini moving?

18. A 10 g bullet travelling at 200 m/s strikes and remains embedded in a 2 kg target, which is originally at rest but free to move. At what speed does the target move off?

19. An aircraft is flying horizontally when it fires a 50 kg projectile directly forward. If the plane, originally flying at 100 m/s, has a mass of 7000 kg and the projectile velocity is 400 m/s relative to the ground, find the plane's velocity immediately after firing the projectile.

20. A proton travelling at 10^7 m/s collides with a stationary particle and bounces back at 6×10^6 m/s. If the particle moves forward at 4×10^6 m/s, find its mass, assuming the proton mass is $1·67 \times 10^{-27}$ kg. What might this particle be? (See Book 1, page 50f).

21. A boy of mass 60 kg running at 6 m/s jumps on to a stationary 5 kg sledge and both move off along level ice. If the frictional force is 50 newtons, how long will it take for them to come to rest?

22. A small car (mass = 500 kg) fails to stop at the entrance to a major road until it has reached the middle of the carriageway. It is then struck by a sports car (mass = 1000 kg) and the two cars lock together. Police investigations show that the skid marks stretch for 40 m. Assuming that the frictional force on these two vehicles was constant at $7·5 \times 10^3$ newtons, find

  (a) the deceleration of the two cars
  (b) the speed at which the two cars moved off after the impact
  (c) the speed of the sports car just before the impact—in miles per hour (100 mi/h = 45 m/s approx.).

Interaction

You have already seen that forces occur in pairs—action and reaction. (Book 1, chapter 11). Remember that these forces never act on the *same* body; it is always a matter of A acting on B and B acting on A.

Experiment 7.8. Insert a steel projectile into the plunger of a trolley. Load the plunger and release it (Fig. 145). Describe the forces acting on the trolley and the projectile.

Repeat the experiment using a wooden projectile. What differences do you observe?

Finally release the loaded plunger with no projectile in it. What happens? What force was exerted on the trolley?

Fig. 145

This experiment shows us that, although in every case the spring had exactly the same tension (and the same potential energy), the force exerted on the trolley when it was released varied. The force exerted *on* the trolley was dependent on the force exerted *by* the trolley. If there was nothing on which the trolley could exert a force, no force could be exerted on the trolley. This being so, it is better to regard force as an *interaction* between two bodies rather than think of action and reaction as two separate forces. This force of interaction acts equally in opposite directions and 'action' and 'reaction' are merely labels to identify them. As they act *together* they should not be thought of as cause and effect. If you look at the collision in Fig. 141, this can be seen clearly. As the moving puck approaches the stationary one interaction occurs. It is not a matter of the moving puck pushing the stationary one (action) and then the stationary one responding by pushing the moving one (reaction): they both push each other at the same time. A pushes B and B pushes A. This is interaction. Newton himself made the point clear when discussing the planets. He said 'It is not one action by which the sun attracts Jupiter and another by which Jupiter attracts the sun: but it is *one action* by which the sun and Jupiter mutually endeavour to approach each other'.

Here are a few simple experiments to illustrate Newton's Third Law.

Project 7.9.

(*a*) A circular track of 26 in diameter made from six Hornby rails is placed on a bicycle wheel (Fig. 146).

(*b*) Place a Sparklet bulb in the central tube of a trolley and pierce the end of the bulb. Alternatively fix the bulb to a vehicle on a linear air track!

(*c*) Fix a bicycle valve into the stopper of a liquid soap bottle (polythene). Half fill the bottle with water and make sure the stopper

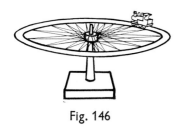

Fig. 146

Fig. 147

is fitted tightly. Set up the apparatus as shown in Fig. 147 and pump air into the bottle. The experiment should be conducted in a playground!

(*d*) Try to discover all you can about jet engines and rockets and paste some photographs and diagrams into your lab. book.

Fig. 148

From the Esso film "Momentum and Collision Processes"

(*e*) What will happen (i) when the girl holds the rope and the boy, of equal mass, pulls (Fig. 148)? (ii) when the boy holds the rope and the girl pulls? and (ii) when both boy and girl pull the rope at the same time?

Momentum and Newton's Third Law

In the experiment with the exploding trolleys (Experiment 7.3, page 79) we discovered that momentum was conserved. Consider the situation after the trolleys have been moving for a short time (Δt). We will assume that they have reached speeds of v and v'. If we take motion to the right as *positive*, then the changes of velocity (from rest) are $-\Delta v$ and $\Delta v'$ respectively

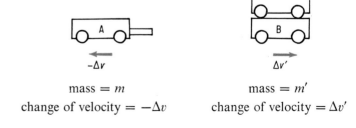

mass $= m$ mass $= m'$

change of velocity $= -\Delta v$ change of velocity $= \Delta v'$

From the experimental results:

$$-m\Delta v = m'\Delta v'$$

As each change of momentum took place in the same time (Δt)

$$-m\frac{\Delta v}{\Delta t} = m'\frac{\Delta v'}{\Delta t}$$

or $-ma = m'a'$

So from Newton's Second Law

$$-F = F'$$

The force A exerts on B is thus *equal in magnitude and opposite in direction* to the force B exerts on A. This is Newton's Third Law and the conservation of momentum is really another way of stating the law. Newton's Third Law tells us that when two bodies *interact* the forces they exert on each other are equal in magnitude and opposite in direction.

Gravitational Interaction

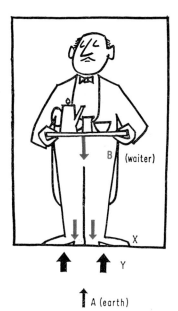

A waiter stands on a floor: what forces act on him? The Earth pulls him downwards and the floor pushes him upwards. If these forces are equal (and opposite) he will be in equilibrium. These are *not*, however, forces of action and reaction. In the first place both forces act on *one* body—the waiter—but Newton 3 forces always act on different bodies. Secondly we cannot describe these forces in terms of A acting on B and B acting on A. If we consider the force which the Earth exerts on the waiter (weight) as the action, then the reaction must be the force the waiter exerts on the Earth. *Does the waiter really pull the Earth towards him?* (23) *If he were to jump off the floor would he push the Earth away from him with the same force as the Earth exerted on him?* (24) *Would momentum be conserved?* (25)

Fig. 150

If now we consider the forces the waiter exerts on the floor (X in Fig. 150) as the action, then the reaction must be the force the floor exerts on the waiter (Y). It is true that under normal circumstances B and X are equal. Each equals the weight of the waiter. If, however, the floor on which he was standing happened to be the floor of a lift, B and X would be the same only when the lift was at rest or travelling at a constant speed. In the extreme case (Fig. 95, Book 2) X and Y would disappear, but B would still be equal to A and would still have the same value as before.

A free-fall laboratory has recently been constructed in the Department of Aeronautics of Glasgow University. The small laboratory falls through a 5-storey building thus enabling engineers to take measurements under free-fall conditions.

Project 7.10. Place a heavy block of metal on a board and stretch an elastic thread round it as shown in Fig. 151. Why does the block not move? Now drop the board. Did the interaction between block and board disappear whilst they were falling? Did the block lose its mass while it fell? Did the gravitational attraction (weight) disappear?

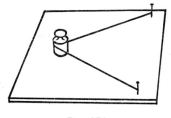

Fig. 151

Problems on Newton's Third Law of Motion

26. *If you blow up a toy balloon and throw it in the air without closing its mouth, what happens and why?*

27. *If the following forces are labelled 'action', state the 'reaction' for each. Give its direction and say what it acts on.*

(a) *the pull (east) of 6 boys on a tug-of-war rope.*
(b) *the push (clockwise) of water on a rotating garden sprinkler.*
(c) *the gravitational pull (down) on a falling parachutist.*
(d) *the pull (down) of the Earth on a satellite.*
(e) *the pull (up) of a coalman on a bag of coal.*
(f) *the force (north) of a cricket bat on a ball originally moving southwards.*

28. *When a ball (mass = 0·6 kg) is dropped it accelerates towards the Earth (mass = 6 × 10²⁴ kg). If the ball accelerates at 10 m/s² find the Earth's acceleration.*

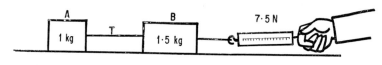

Fig. 152

29. *Two frictionless pucks are tied together by a thread (T) and pulled by a spring balance reading 7·5 newtons. If the pucks have masses of 1 kg and 1·5 kg respectively (Fig. 152), find*

(a) *the tension of the string joining them,*
(b) *the unbalanced force acting on each puck,*
(c) *the force A exerts on the thread,*
(d) *the force the thread exerts on A,*
(e) *the force B exerts on the thread (T), and*
(f) *the force the thread (T) exerts on B.*

30. *Explain how the following are propelled—*

(a) *a propeller-driven ship,*
(b) *a sailing ship,*
(c) *a jet plane,*
(d) *a rocket, and*
(e) *a car.*

31. *If you were becalmed in a sailing boat and you had a powerful blower on board, could you propel the boat by*
(a) *blowing against the sails, or*
(b) *directing the nozzle over the stern?*

32. *Explain why you cannot pull yourself up by your shoe laces.*

33. *A 1 kg mass is hung on a spring balance. The mass is pulled down until the balance reads 15 newtons. If the mass is released find its initial acceleration, assuming g = 10 m/s².*

34. *A jet engine takes in 20 kg of air per second at 100 m/s. After being compressed and heated the air is discharged at 500 m/s. Calculate the thrust of the engine.*

35. *A 1 kg mass is moving horizontally at 500 m/s. Can you calculate what force it will exert on a stone wall? (Think twice about this!)*

Optional Extras

Momentum and Relative Velocity

If you imagine yourself sitting on one of two moving trolleys, then the velocity at which the other is approaching you or going away from you is called the *relative velocity* of that trolley with respect to you. In Experiment 7.1, page 76, the two trolleys moved off together with the same velocity after the collision. Their relative velocity was then zero. A collision of this kind is said to be completely *inelastic*. In Experiment 7.2 you found the velocities and the momenta before and after an *elastic* collision. *Can you find the relative velocities before and after each collision?* (36)

When the relative velocity after an impact is *numerically* the same as it was before the impact, the collision is said to be *completely elastic. Why is it necessary to say* 'numerically *the same*'*?* (37)

Problem 38. *A 100 gram marble travelling 1 m/s strikes a stationary 25 gram marble. What was their relative velocity before the collision?*

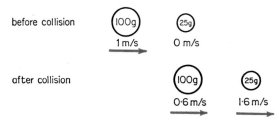

Fig. 153

After the impact the larger marble is slowed down to 0·6 m/s and the small one shoots off at 1·6 m/s. What is their relative velocity now? Is it a velocity of approach or separation? What was the total momentum before and after the collision? What kind of collision is this?

Project 7.11. Fix a piece of aluminium foil to the side of a football and suspend the ball by a long wire which makes electrical contact with the foil. The other end of the wire should be connected to a scaler which can be used as an electric stop-clock.

Fix another piece of foil to the toe of a boy's boot and wire this to the other 'make to count' contact of the scaler (Fig. 154). When the boot is in contact with the ball the scaler operates and records the time of contact.

An electric stop clock or another scaler switched photo-electrically can be used to find the velocity of the ball after it has been kicked.

Zero both timing devices, kick the ball, and find the time of impact (Δt). From the time taken for the ball to pass through the light beam find the velocity (v) of the ball.

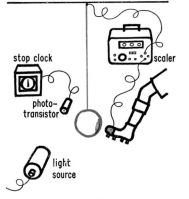

Fig. 154

If the ball in the last experiment reached a velocity (v) after being kicked, its acceleration would be

$$\frac{v - 0}{\Delta t}$$

Calling the change of velocity Δv we have

$$\text{acceleration} = \frac{\Delta v}{\Delta t}$$

If the mass of the ball is m grams its change of momentum is $m.\Delta v$, and from Newton's Second Law

$$F = ma = m\frac{\Delta v}{\Delta t} = \frac{\text{change of momentum}}{\text{time interval}}$$

We see then that Newton's second law equates force with the change of momentum every second (that is, the *rate* of change of momentum). In fact this was how Newton originally stated his law.

From the above equation we see that

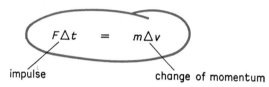

impulse   change of momentum

The change of momentum is equal to $F \times \Delta t$, which is the impulse of the force, or simply the *impulse*.

Can you now find the average value of the force (F) acting between the boot and the ball in Project 7.11? (39)

When dealing with graphs of velocity and time what did the area *under the curve represent? (40)* If we now plot force against time the area represents *impulse*. As we are normally considering a small time interval the area is a tall narrow strip. If we assume the force to be constant (which it normally is not!) the graph would look like Fig. 155.

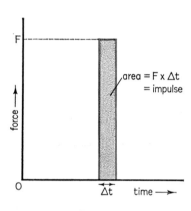

Fig. 155

Practical Puzzles

41. *Place a sheet of carbon paper on top of white paper on the floor. Allow a ball bearing to drop from Position A (Fig. 156) so that it marks the paper on the floor. Now roll the ball down the slope₃ so that it rolls off the table, lands on the paper, and leaves a mark. Calculate the velocity of the ball at A, from the distances h and d.*

Finally place one ball bearing at position B and allow one identical ball to roll down the slope from the same height as before. Note where both ball bearings fall. Calculate the velocities of the balls when they separated at AB. How could this experiment be used to verify the conservation of momentum?

In an experiment like this ball B has a mass of 30 g, h is 1·25 m and d is 1·5 m. Find (a) the time taken for A to fall, (b) the velocity at which B leaves A, (c) the momentum of B as it leaves A, (d) the impulse during the impact, (e) the average acceleration of the ball if the impact lasts 50 microseconds, (f) the average force acting during the impact, and (g) the velocity of B just before it lands. Give its magnitude and direction.

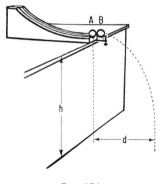

Fig. 156

42. *Weigh a hammer and estimate the mass of its head. Devise a method of estimating the speed at which the head is moving when it strikes a nail. Now use the hammer to knock a nail into a board*

but connect the nail and hammer head to a scaler and time the impact. Calculate the average force exerted.

A hammer head of mass 1 kg is moving at 3 m/s when it strikes a nail. If the rebound velocity is zero, and the impact lasts for 15 milli-seconds, find the impulse and the average force exerted.

43. (a) *A trolley fitted with a spring-loaded plunger is placed at one end of a long trolley as shown in Fig. 157. A needle in the small trolley can penetrate a lump of plasticine fixed to the opposite end of the long trolley. When the plunger is released the long trolley moves 15 cm to the right. The distance from the needle to the plasticine is 45 cm. If the small trolley has a mass of 750 g, what is the mass of the long trolley? You may ignore frictional forces.*

Think very carefully; this is not quite as simple as it looks!

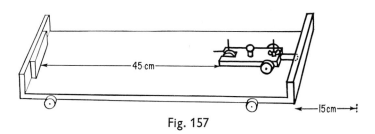

Fig. 157

(b) *Using the apparatus shown in Fig. 157 load the small trolley until both trolleys have the same mass. Use the aluminium nose of the small trolley and a rubber band on the larger trolley to provide an elastic collision. Describe what happens when the small trolley is given a push along the top of the other and collides* elastically *with it.*

Additional Problems

44. *The ram of a pile-driver has a mass of 500 kg. If it is raised above the Earth's surface and released,*

    (a) *what force acts on the ram?*
    (b) *what force acts on the Earth?*
    (c) *does the Earth move towards the ram?*
    (d) *what is the acceleration of the ram with respect to the Earth?*
    (e) *what is the velocity of the ram after dropping for 0·8 second?*
    (f) *what is its momentum after that time?*
    (g) *does the Earth have the same (i) acceleration, (ii) velocity, or (iii) momentum as the ram? What frame of reference are you using?*

45. *Three trolleys are pulled down a friction-compensated slope by a force of 1 newton (Fig. 158). Find the tensions in the strings (T_1 and T_2).*

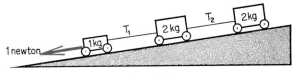

Fig. 158

46. *An unbalanced force is applied for 2 seconds to a mass of 4 kg originally at rest. If the mass moves 10 metres in that time, find*

(a) *the acceleration of the mass,*
(b) *the speed at the end of the two seconds,*
(c) *the impulse applied to the body, and*
(d) *the change of momentum.*

47. *A skier of mass 60 kg runs into a bank of snow and is brought to rest in 2 seconds. If he was travelling at 12 m/s, find (a) the average force exerted by the snow on the skier, (b) the average force exerted by the skier on the snow and (c) the impulse.*

48. *A car of mass 1500 kg has a maximum braking force of 7000 N. Find (a) the maximum deceleration possible, (b) the distance gone before stopping from speeds of 4·5 m/s (10 mi/h), 18 m/s (40 mi/h) and 45 m/s (100 mi/h).*

49. *A boy of mass 50 kg is travelling at 3 m/s on a playground trolley of mass 20 kg. The boy jumps off the back of the trolley and in doing so applies a force to it for 0·15 seconds, thus giving it a forward impulse of 15 newton-seconds. Find*

(a) *the average force applied to the trolley by the boy,*
(b) *the final speed of the trolley, and*
(c) *the horizontal velocity with which the boy lands.*

50. *A ball of mass 0·6 kg travelling at 10 m/s (east) strikes a wall perpendicularly and rebounds at 9 m/s (west). The impact lasts 0·05 seconds.*

(a) *What was the original momentum of the ball?*
(b) *What was the change of momentum of the ball?*
(c) *What was the impulse on the wall?*
(d) *What was the average force acting on the wall?*
(e) *What was the average force acting on the ball?*

51. *A football of mass 0·5 kg reaches a velocity of 20 m/s (east) after a kick lasting 0·02 seconds. Find*

(a) *the impulse,*
(b) *the change of momentum of the ball,*
(c) *the average force exerted on the ball, and*
(d) *the displacement of the ball in 3 seconds.*

What assumption must you make to answer the last question? Do you think the error would be insignificant or fairly large? Under what conditions could the error be very large?

52. *Normally, the fuel in a rocket accounts for nearly all its mass. The payload can be compared to the shell of an egg and the fuel to the entire contents. The dummy Apollo capsule plus the shell of the second-stage rocket had a mass of 8×10^3 kg, whereas the combined lift-off mass of the capsule and Saturn two-stage rocket was $5·7 \times 10^5$ kg. If the thrust generated by the booster rocket was $6·7 \times 10^6$ newtons, find*

(a) *the unbalanced force acting on the rocket, and*
(b) *the vertical acceleration of the rocket initially. Neglect air resistance—but* not *gravity!*

Fig. 159

53. A boy and a girl of equal mass hang on either end of a rope which passes over a frictionless pulley (Fig. 159). If the boy starts to climb the rope who will reach the pulley first? Explain the answer you give.

54. A 1 kg trolley moving at 2 m/s collides and sticks to another 1 kg trolley originally at rest. At what speed do they move off?

The experiment is now repeated with a powerful magnet fixed to one end of each trolley so that they accelerate towards each other. How will this affect (a) their relative velocity before impact (b) the total momentum after impact?

Visual Aids

8 mm Cassettes: Translational acceleration$_{18}$.
16 mm Films: Laws of Motion$_{23}$ 21.7331.
        Rockets, How they Work$_{23}$ 21.7218.
        Frames of reference (P.S.S.C.)$_{26}$ 3D.2638.
        Momentum and Collision processes$_{28}$ (for teachers).

More Work

CHAPTER 8

Energy

The study of energy and its changes from one form to another is an important concern of physics. In an earlier part of the course (Book 1, chapter 13) we discussed many of these different forms. *Can you name some of them?* (1) *Can you trace the origin of every type of energy to the sun?* (2) *What is the ultimate fate of each type of energy?* (3)

When we buy energy for our bodies, homes or cars we usually get it in a chemical or electrical form. The ease with which electrical energy can be changed to so many other forms causes the demand for electrical energy to increase each year. At present British power stations can supply about 40,000 megawatts (4×10^{10} W), but this is expected to be doubled by the early 1970's. *What forms of energy are used to operate these power stations?* (4)

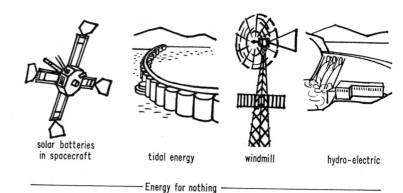

solar batteries
in spacecraft   tidal energy   windmill   hydro-electric

——————— Energy for nothing ———————

Fig. 160

Mechanical energy may also be readily changed into many other forms. In addition to the ordinary uses of mechanical energy in transport and industry, all our electrical generators are, at present, mechanically driven. It is with mechanical energy that this chapter is mainly concerned.

Problems

5. *Devices used to change energy from one form to another are called* transducers. *Name transducers which change*

   (a) *sound to electrical energy,*
   (b) *electrical energy to sound,*
   (c) *light to electrical energy,*

96

Atlas   Woman lifting   Earth
              poodle   satellite

Fig. 161

(d) *electrical energy to light,*
(e) *chemical energy to electrical energy,*
(f) *heat to mechanical energy,*
(g) *electrical energy to mechanical energy.*

6. *Does an electro-magnet use energy to hold up an iron block? Would a permanent magnet use energy to do this?*

7. *Is work being done in any of the cases illustrated in Fig. 161?*

Work

Energy is required to move a stationary body. *Once the body is moving, is energy always required to keep it moving at a steady speed? (8) Explain your answer. (9)*

If a force (F) acts on a body and moves it a distance (d) in the direction in which the force is acting, we measure the energy transfer (work done) by the product $F \times d$.

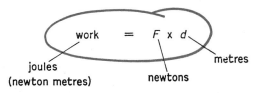

This, in fact, defines the energy unit in the international system (SI). The *joule* is a *newton metre*, that is, it is the work done when a force of 1 newton acts through 1 metre. J. P. Joule (1818–1889) did some of the first precise experiments to measure energy transfer. We will see later that the joule is now used to measure all forms of energy. The work done in lifting an apple from the floor on to a table is about 1 joule. In a hard day's work a man might dissipate about 1 million joules (1 megajoule).

If you push a lawnmower for 10 minutes, you may say that you have done twice as much work as you did in 5 minutes. This may well be true. Is the amount of work done, then, proportional to the product of force and time? Why do we define work as force × distance and not force × time?

To answer this we must ask if work is *always* done when a force acts for a certain time. A bird sitting on a telegraph wire is exerting a force on the wire. *Is any energy being transferred? (10) Does it do twice as much work if it sits there twice as long? (11)* Only in the special case of a force pushing a body at a *constant speed* (e.g. the lawnmower) is the work done proportional to the time, and this is simply because *in this case* time and distance are proportional.

Problems

12. *A cable car is pulled by a force of 6 × 10³ newtons. Travelling at 4 m/s it takes 200 s to reach the top of a hill. How much work is done?*

13. *Two 50-centimetre lengths of rubber, one thick and one thin, are each stretched by 20 centimetres. Discuss the forces acting on each and the work done in each case. If the same force had been applied to each what would have happened?*

14. *As the moon circles the Earth an unbalanced force is acting on it pulling it towards the Earth. A force acts on the moon and the moon is moving yet no work is done. Why not?*

Machines

If the force acting on one side of a balanced arm is multiplied by the distance from the fulcrum, it is exactly equal to a similar product on the other side. In other words (Fig. 162).

$$f \times A = F \times a$$
$$5 \times 6 = 10 \times 3$$
$$30 \quad = \quad 30$$

As this product is constant it has been given a special name—the *moment* of the force. We call the products *fA* and *Fa* the anti-clockwise and clockwise *moments about 0*.

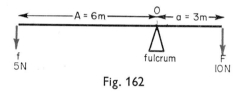

Fig. 162

If *f* is pushed down a distance *D* so that *F* is raised by *d* we find that (very nearly)

$$f \times D = F \times d$$

What do these products represent? (15)

Can you get more out of a machine than you put in? This is a vague question! If it means more *energy*, the answer is 'no', otherwise some of the output of energy could be fed back into the input and the machine would go on for ever.

If the above question means more *force* the answer is 'yes'. In fact the object of using a machine is usually to produce a greater force than would be otherwise available. Machines can also change the direction in which a force acts. One of the simplest machines is the lever.

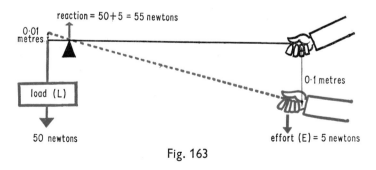

Fig. 163

Imagine a weightless lever pivoted as shown in Fig. 163. A load (*L*) exerts a weight of 50 newtons on one end, and an effort (*E*) of

5 newtons applied to the other end is needed to raise the load. The load is $\frac{5}{50} = 10$ times greater than the effort. *What is this ratio $\frac{L}{E}$ called?* (16) (Book 1, page 114).

If the effort moves through 0·1 metres in 1 second its velocity is 0·1 metres/second. If the load is raised 0·01 metres in that time its velocity is 0·01 metres/second. The ratio is therefore $\frac{0·1}{0·01} = 10$.

What is this ratio called? (17) Let us find the work obtained from the machine and the work put into the machine.

$$\begin{aligned}
\text{output} &= \text{potential energy gained by the load} \\
&= \text{load} \times \text{distance load is raised} \\
&= L \times d_l \\
&= 50 \text{ newtons} \times 0·01 \text{ metres} \\
&= 0·5 \text{ joules} \\
\text{input} &= \text{work done by the effort} \\
&= \text{effort} \times \text{distance effort moves} \\
&= E \times d_e \\
&= 5 \text{ newtons} \times 0·1 \text{ metres} \\
&= 0·5 \text{ joules}
\end{aligned}$$

No real machine would ever have quite as big an output of energy as its input. *Why is this?* (18)

The ratio of output/input is called the *efficiency* of the machine. It is usually expressed as a percentage.

$$\text{efficiency} = \frac{\text{energy output}}{\text{energy input}} \times 100\%$$

Remembering that $MA = \frac{L}{E}$ *and* $VR = \frac{d_e}{d_l}$ *can you deduce a numerical relationship between MA, VR and efficiency?* (19)

Practical Puzzles

20. *A uniform rod has a mass of Y kg. If it is balanced horizontally and attached to a spring balance as shown in Fig. 164, find the value of X, Y and Z. Mark, in newtons, all the forces acting on*

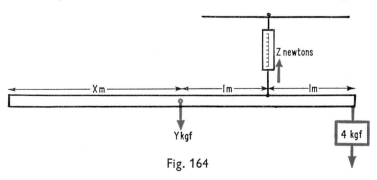

Fig. 164

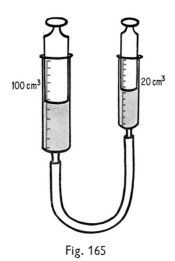

Fig. 165

the rod and indicate the direction in which they act. *If the point of suspension were moved to the centre of gravity of the rod, how could balance be regained?*

21. *If you were given a knife, some string, a 1 kg mass and a metre rule, describe* in detail *how you could find the mass of a retort stand.*

22. *A model of a hydraulic lift can be constructed from two syringes. What is the velocity ratio of the machine illustrated in Fig. 165? How could you find its mechanical advantage and efficiency?*

Problems

23. *If the bar shown in Fig. 163 had a mass of 0·5 kilograms and its centre of gravity was 50 centimetres to the right of the pivot, find the MA, VR and efficiency of the machine when used to lift the same load. Assume that there is no friction at the pivot. Can you explain this amazing result?*

24. *Why have tinsmiths' shears long handles and short blades and tailors' shears short handles and long blades?*

25. *How could you use a pound of butter and a broomstick to estimate the weight of a bag of apples? Describe fully exactly what you would do and what measurements you would take.*

26. *Describe how a wheel and axle may be regarded as a form of lever (cf. Book 1, page 115).*

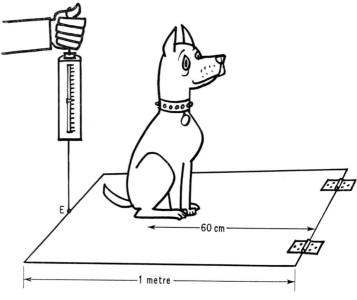

Fig. 166

27. *A dog (mass = 4 kg) sits 60 cm from the hinge of a uniform horizontal trap door (mass = 6 kg). If a vertical force is exerted at the edge of the trap door (Fig. 166), find*

(a) *the force needed to raise the door (ignoring friction),*
(b) *the potential energy gained by the dog if it is raised 6 cm,*

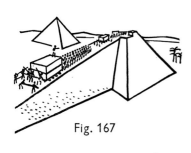

Fig. 167

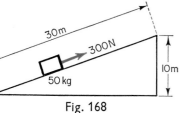

Fig. 168

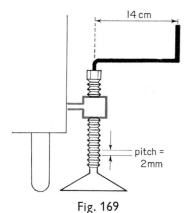

Fig. 169

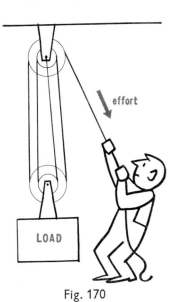

Fig. 170

(c) how far the edge of the door (E) is raised in order to raise the dog 6 cm,

(d) the mechanical advantage of the system (ignoring friction).

28. *Would you expect the diameter of a brake disc fitted to a sports car to be greater or less than that used in a small saloon car? Why? Why do the brakes get hot?*

Pyramids, Ramps, Wedges and Screws

It is thought that a huge inclined plane was used during the construction of the Great Pyramid near Cairo. Over two million limestone blocks were used to build the Pyramid, each having a mass of more than 2 tons. 100,000 slaves are estimated to have worked for 20 years to build it. Today the principle of the inclined plane is used in ramps, wedges and screws.

Project 8.1. Can you find the velocity ratio of a vice or a G-clamp? How would you try to find its mechanical advantage and efficiency for a certain load?

Practical Puzzle 29. If a mass of 50 kg is pushed up an incline of 1 in 3 (Fig. 168) by an applied force of 300 newtons, find (a) the VR, (b) the MA and (c) the efficiency of the inclined plane. How did you define the VR?

Can you devise a model inclined plane in which you can measure the effort and hence find the MA and efficiency? Sketch the practical arrangement. How is the efficiency affected if the load is placed on rollers or wheels? Explain the difference.

Problems

30. *A ramp is 4 metres long and one end is 1 metre higher than the other. If a force of 300 newtons parallel to the ramp is needed to slide an 80 kg box up at a constant speed,*

(a) find the work done by the effort in moving the box up the plane.
(b) find the potential energy gained by the box.
(c) why are the above answers not the same?
(d) find the MA, VR and efficiency of this machine.

31. *For what purposes are screws with fine threads preferable to screws with coarse threads?*

32. *Find the velocity ratio of the jack illustrated in Fig. 169. Take π as $\frac{22}{7}$. What might be the efficiency of a jack like this?*

Pulleys

The block and tackle is one of the simplest forms of pulley system. Its velocity ratio depends on the number of wheels in each block and the particular way the system is used. To find the velocity ratio imagine the load moved through 1 metre and work out how far the effort has to move. *What is the velocity ratio of the system illustrated in Fig. 170?* (33)

Experiment 8.2. Using a block and tackle system of pulleys, a wheel and axle or any other machine, find the VR and MA for a number of different loads. Plot a graph showing how the efficiency varies with the load. Can you suggest any reason for the slope of graph you obtain?

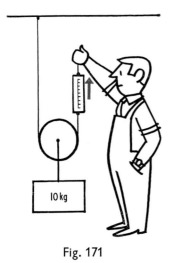

Fig. 171

Problems

34. *In the arrangement shown in Fig. 171 what will the spring balance read when it is stationary? What assumptions are you making? How will the reading alter if the load is (a) accelerated upwards (b) raised at a constant speed?*

35. *A man of mass 70 kg has to lift a weight of 3×10^3 newtons. What is the smallest VR possible? Draw a possible pulley system and mark the tension in each rope. If the man can just raise the load by dangling on the effort rope, find the MA of the machine and its efficiency.*

36. *If you wanted to exert the greatest possible force on a car, would you use the pulleys as shown in Fig. 172 (a) or as in (b)? Why? What is the velocity ratio in each case?*

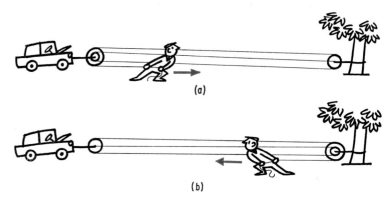

(a)

(b)

Fig. 172

37. *In a machine the following results were obtained.*

Load (newtons)	10	30	60	100
Effort (newtons)	1·9	3·1	5	7·5

Draw a graph showing the effort/load. Find the MA in each case and draw a graph showing MA/load. What would be the shape of the graph of efficiency/load? Assuming the machine to be, at best, about 50 per cent efficient, what might be its velocity ratio?

Power

A Jaguar is more *powerful* than a Mini. What does this mean? If we take petrol consumption as a rough estimate of energy transfer, we might find that the Jaguar used five times as much petrol as the Mini *in one hour.* It is important to mention the time, as clearly a Mini travelling for 10 hours is likely to use more petrol than a Jaguar travelling for 10 minutes. Power, then, depends on energy transfer (that is, work done) in a given time. In the case of a car the petrol consumption might express the *input*, and the work done against friction, air resistance, and gravity would represent the *output*. The brake horse power rating of a car refers to the output.

$$\text{Power} = \frac{\text{work done}}{\text{time}}$$

When James Watt of Greenock developed his steam engine nearly 200 years ago, people wanted to know how many horses it would replace. Consequently he arranged that a cart horse should pull a mass of 100 lbs up a mine shaft. He found that the horse moved at about $3\frac{2}{3}$ feet per second. To be on the safe side, when promising how powerful *his* engines would be, he assumed that a really powerful horse might move at $5\frac{1}{2}$ feet per second thus giving 550 ft lbf/s as *one horse-power*. This is, of course, a purely arbitrary figure and, although it is still used in Britain for some purposes, we will use the simpler unit named in honour of James Watt. The *watt* is a power of one joule per second. To get some idea of the connection between watts and horse-power consider this example. The maximum power developed by a Mini is 34 horse-power, which is about 25,000 watts (25 kW). One horse-power is about 746 watts.

$$\text{Power} = \frac{\text{work}}{\text{time}} = \frac{\text{force} \times \text{distance}}{\text{time}} = \text{force} \times \text{speed}$$

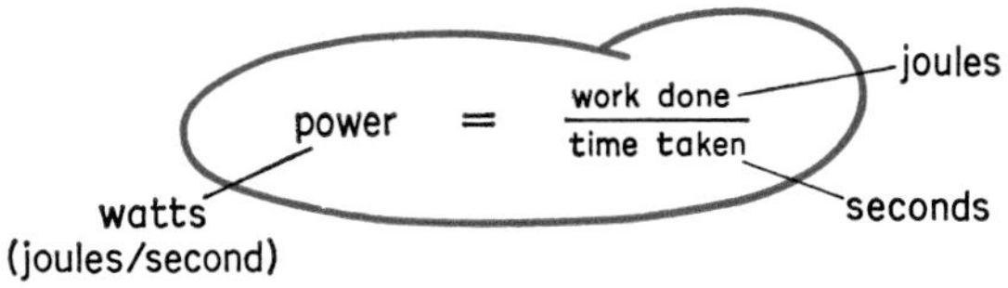

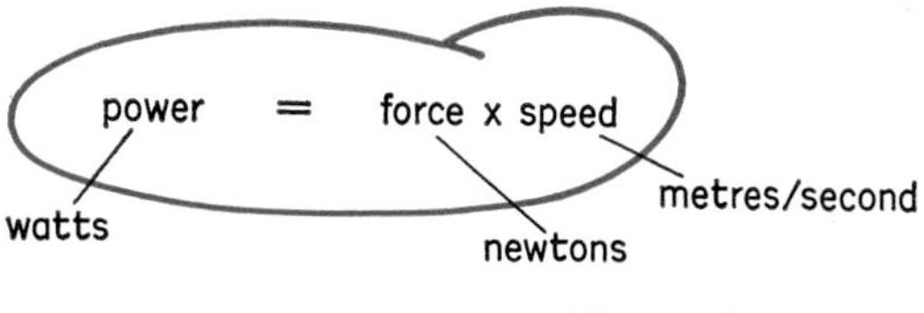

If you walk at a moderate pace you will use about 100 joules of energy every second, that is, 100 watts. On a bicycle you would travel about four times as fast using the same power.

Experiment 8.3. Find your weight in newtons (1 lbf = 4·45 N) and the time taken to run up a flight of stairs. Finally measure the height of the stairs in metres and then calculate your power in watts. Can you work as hard as a one bar (1 kW) electric fire?

Measuring Power

If a chisel is pressed to the surface of a grindstone it gets hot. *Where does the heat energy come from?* (38). *What factors will alter the amount of heat produced?* (39). We could measure the amount of energy being changed to heat if we knew the frictional force acting between the wheel and the chisel and the distance the circumference of the wheel moves.

If we have a belt running over a pulley wheel (Fig. 173) we can measure the force applied when the wheel rotates. Imagine first of all that two spring balances each read 10 N when the wheel is stationary. Clearly the wheel is not exerting a force along the belt.

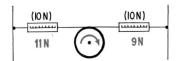

Fig. 173

If, however, the wheel starts to turn in the direction shown, the readings might alter to 11 N and 9 N. *What force is then tending to stop the wheel?* (40). If the circumference of the wheel is 50 cm (0·5 m), then

$$\text{work done for one revolution} = F \times d$$
$$= 2 \times 0\cdot5$$
$$= 1 \text{ joule}$$

If the wheel rotates 30 times a second:

$$\text{power} = \frac{\text{work}}{\text{time}} = \frac{30 \times 1 \text{ joules}}{1 \text{ second}} = 30 \text{ joules/second}$$
$$= 30 \text{ watts.}$$

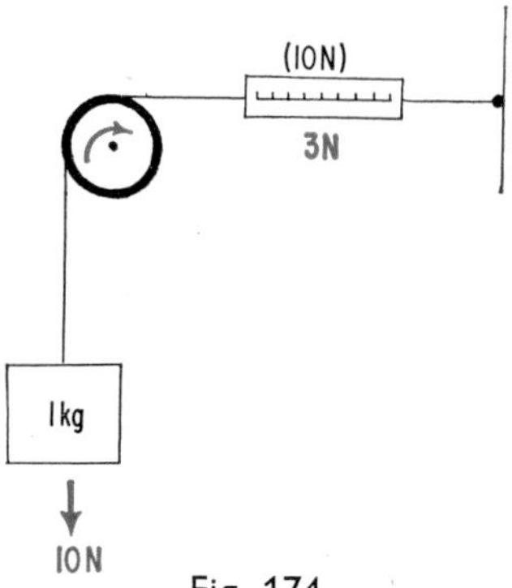

To increase the frictional force applied to the wheel the belt can be wrapped round the wheel (Fig. 174). This will increase the transfer of energy for a given movement of the wheel. In the case illustrated in Fig. 174 only one spring balance is used and the reading is 10 N when the wheel is at rest. With the wheel running the balance reads 3 N so that a force of 7 N is being exerted on the belt. If the circumference is 0·5 m as before, we have

$$\text{work done for 1 revolution} = F \times d$$
$$= 7 \text{ newtons} \times 0\cdot5 \text{ metres}$$
$$= 3\cdot5 \text{ newton metres}$$
$$= 3\cdot5 \text{ joules}$$

If the wheel was rotating at 10 revolutions per second we have

$$\text{power} = \frac{3\cdot5 \times 10}{1} = 35 \text{ watts}$$

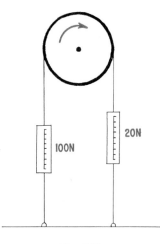

(10N)

3N

1 kg

10N

Fig. 174

Fig. 175

The power delivered by engines (brake horse power) is measured in this way. By altering the load (frictional force acting round the drum) and the speed of the engine the maximum output of the engine can be determined by experiment.

Practical Puzzle 41. *An electric motor drives a wheel over which a belt passes (Fig. 175). If spring balances attached to the belt read 100 N and 20 N respectively when the wheel rotates at 10 revs per second, find the power. The circumference of the wheel is 0·6 metres. If the motor takes 3 amps from a 240 volt mains supply, find the efficiency of the motor.*

Experiment 8.4

(*a*) Try to find the maximum power of a model steam engine by finding the rate at which different masses can be raised.

(*b*) Can you devise an experiment to measure (i) the output power of a bicycle dynamo (amps × volts = watts) and (ii) the input power to the pedals? From these results calculate the efficiency.

Problems

42. *A man can mow a lawn in 30 minutes but his son claims to do the same job in 20 minutes. Does the son do more work? Is his power greater?*

43. *A hydraulic lift raises a car of mass 1·5 × 10³ kilograms by 2 metres in 20 seconds. Find the power (wattage) used.*

44. *At the Niagara Falls water drops about 50 metres. If 7 × 10⁶ kilograms of water fall every second, what power is available at the bottom?*

45. *If the output power of an electric motor is 50 kW, at what speed can it raise a 2000 kg elevator?*

46. *Can a 1 kilowatt engine lift as big a load as a 5 kilowatt engine? Explain your answer.*

47. *A Jaguar rated at 150 kilowatts has a top speed of 50 metres a second on a level road. What is the retarding force?*

Mechanical Energy

1. Potential Energy

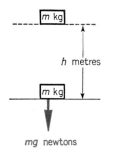

Fig. 176

If a box of mass m kilograms is lying on the floor, a gravitational force of mg newtons is acting on it pulling it downwards (Fig. 176). In order to lift the box it is necessary to apply an upward force of mg newtons to it. In fact, a force very slightly greater than mg newtons is required to start it moving upwards, but we will ignore this as the difference can be extremely small. If the force raises the box h metres vertically, the work done ($F \times d$) is $mg \times h$ joules. Energy has been transformed, and can now be *stored* by placing the box on a ledge h metres above the floor. *Can we recover this energy?* (48) *What happens if the box is knocked off the ledge?* (49) We call this stored energy *gravitational potential energy*, although it is often referred to simply as potential energy (P.E.).

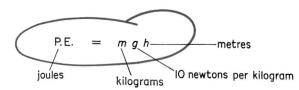

Energy may be stored in the form of gravitational potential energy when generating stations are producing more electrical energy than the consumers require. It is often difficult to reduce the output of a generating plant, and the most economic method of storing the surplus energy is to use it to pump water to a high level loch (Fig. 177). Pumped storage systems of this kind are used at Loch Awe in Scotland, Ffestiniog in Wales, and Vianden in Luxembourg. These systems allow the electricity boards to cope with large changes in the demand which, they say, occur immediately after certain TV programmes, such as 'Miss World'!

Potential energy available from sea water at high tide is being harnessed to produce electricity in the Rance Estuary Scheme in France and at Passamaquoddy in the U.S.A.

Fig. 177

Coil Springs

Mechanical energy can also be stored by deforming or compressing certain elastic materials such as rubber. A stretched elastic band has potential energy which can be released when the band is allowed to contract. You should investigate the bouncing

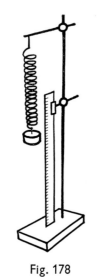

Fig. 178

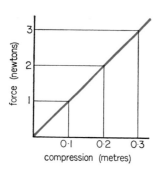

Fig. 179

properties of different rubber balls[21], and try to explain the difference observed in terms of energy transfer. *Can you think of a use for non-bouncy rubber?* (50) *Can you suggest how air in a cylinder (e.g. a syringe) might be used to store energy?* (51) Steel springs will store energy when they are compressed or stretched. *What happens to the energy when a weak spring is stretched so far that it will not spring back?* (52)

Experiment 8.5. Attach various masses to a coil spring and note the *stretch* of the spring in each case (Fig. 178). Do not extend the spring beyond its elastic limit.

Graph your results showing how the stretch (in metres) varies with the force (in newtons). How would you use this graph to illustrate the work done in stretching the spring? Can this elastic potential energy be recovered? How would you find the average force applied to the spring?

Project 8.6. Try to find out how an automatic watch is wound up. In what form is the energy stored during the night?

Problems

53. *The graph in Fig. 179 shows the force needed to compress a coil spring. Find from it (a) the work needed to compress the spring by 20 cm and (b) the potential energy stored in the spring when compressed by 30 cm.*

54. *Give examples of energy stored in magnetic, electric and gravitational fields.*

55. *A man of mass 70 kg jumps to a height of 2 metres. What is his potential energy?*

56. *A rectangular block of metal (density 8 g/cm³) measures 6 × 8 × 8 cm. If it is standing on a square face, what is the minimum energy required to overturn it.*

57. *When a rubber ball strikes a wall it comes to rest for a fraction of a second and then bounces back. Explain the energy changes that take place at each stage. When the ball is at rest how is the energy stored? Explain this in terms of forces between the molecules.*

2. Kinetic Energy

In the following experiments we will use the potential energy stored in a stretched elastic thread to accelerate a vehicle on an air track. We will assume that all the potential energy in the elastic is transformed into kinetic energy in the vehicle, and then try to see how the kinetic energy of a moving body is related (*a*) to its speed and (*b*) to its mass.

Demonstration 8.7.

(*a*) *Speed and Kinetic Energy (Mass Constant).*

Attach a piece of aluminium to an air-track vehicle as shown in Fig. 180. This serves two purposes. First it interrupts the light falling on a photo-transistor and enables the speed of the vehicle to be found, and secondly it enables us to catapult the vehicle by means of one or more elastic threads[3]. The threads used to pull trolleys are suitable for this experiment.

Fix one elastic thread between two uprights as shown in Fig. 180 and use this to propel the vehicles. Note the time taken to pass through the light beam.

Repeat this experiment with other elastic threads—making sure that the vehicle is pulled back to the same place each time—and select four elastic threads which produce the same vehicle speed.

Now find the speed of the vehicle when 1, 2, 3 and then 4 threads are used in parallel: that is for 1, 2, 3 and 4 units of energy. Plot a graph showing speed against energy, then speed squared against energy. What do your graphs suggest?

Fig. 180

(*b*) *Mass and Kinetic Energy* (*Speed Constant*)

For this experiment you will require three additional vehicles each having the same mass as the above vehicle complete with its aluminium plate. Plasticine can be used to load the vehicles.

Use 1 elastic thread and 1 vehicle and note the time of transit. Now place 2 threads on the uprights and see how many vehicles have to be added, end to end, to obtain the same speed as before. Now repeat the process with 3 and then 4 elastic threads.

How are the mass (number of vehicles) and energy (number of elastic threads) related?

Project 8.8. A photo-transistor$_8$ and a powerful beam of light$_3$ can be used in conjunction with a scaler to find the speed of a pendulum bob as it passes the lowest point of its swing (Fig. 181).

Pull the bob aside and, when it is 1 cm above its lowest point, release it. What happens to the potential energy it possessed? What is its potential energy as it passes the light beam?

Repeat this procedure with the bob raised to heights of 4 cm and 9 cm, and then investigate the relationship between height and speed.

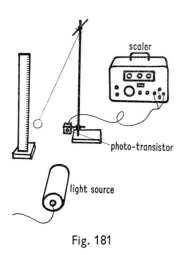

scaler

photo-transistor

light source

Fig. 181

From the last experiments the kinetic energy of a body is seen to be directly proportional to the mass and the square of the speed. If your mathematics is good enough you can see why this must be so!

Let us assume that an unbalanced constant force of F newtons is applied to a stationary box of mass m kilograms (Fig. 182). The box will accelerate at F/m metres per second^2. If the constant force

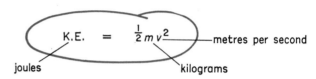

Fig. 182

continues to act so that the box moves through a distance of d metres, then

$$\text{work} = F \times d \text{ joules.}$$

As $F = ma$ and $v^2 = 2\,ad$, we have

$$\text{work} = F \times d$$

$$= ma \times \frac{v^2}{2a}$$

Therefore work $= \frac{1}{2}\,mv^2$ joules

The work done in accelerating the box has been transformed to energy of movement (kinetic energy).

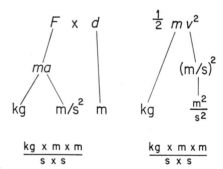

We can show that the units used for work (Fd) and kinetic energy ($\frac{1}{2}\,mv^2$) are the same.

$$F \times d \qquad \frac{1}{2}\,m\,v^2$$

$$\frac{kg \times m \times m}{s \times s} \qquad \frac{kg \times m \times m}{s \times s}$$

If an unbalanced force of 5 newtons acts on a mass of 2 kilograms which is moving at 1 metre per second on a horizontal frictionless table, the acceleration produced will be $\dfrac{F}{m} = 2 \cdot 5$ m/s². By the time the mass has moved 16 metres the velocity has increased to 9 metres per second (Fig. 183).

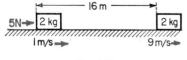

Fig. 183

Initial KE $= \frac{1}{2}\,mv^2 = \frac{1}{2} \times 2 \times 1^2 = \;\;1$ joule

Final KE $\;\;= \frac{1}{2}\,mv^2 = \frac{1}{2} \times 2 \times 9^2 = 81$ joules

Therefore change in kinetic energy $= 80$ joules

Work done $\;\;= F \times d = 5 \times 16 = 80$ joules

In this case all the work put in has been used to increase the kinetic energy of the mass.

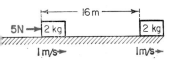

Fig. 184

Fig. 185

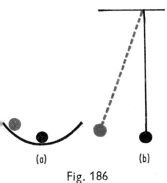

(a)   (b)

Fig. 186

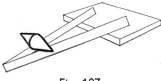

Fig. 187

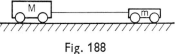

Fig. 188

Now consider the same situation except that the mass now rests on a rough surface which exerts a frictional force of 5 newtons. There is no unbalanced force acting and therefore no acceleration (Fig. 184). The body moves at a steady speed.

$$\text{Original KE} = \tfrac{1}{2}\,mv^2 \qquad\qquad = 1 \text{ joule}$$
$$\text{Final KE} \quad = \tfrac{1}{2}\,mv^2 \qquad\qquad = 1 \text{ joule}$$
$$\text{Therefore change in kinetic energy} = 0$$
$$\text{Work done} = F \times d = 5 \times 16 \quad = 80 \text{ joules}$$

The same amount of energy has been put into the system as before, but this time there is no increase in kinetic energy of the mass. *What has happened to the 80 joules put in?* (58)

Project 8.9. Do you have sufficient faith in the conservation of energy principle to stand with your head against a wall, release a heavy pendulum bob which is touching your nose and remain in the same spot as the bob returns to your nose? Could it bash your nose if the string broke? Explain the results in terms of the conservation of energy. *Warning*—don't push-start the ball!

Project 8.10. Allow a ball bearing to run to and fro on a piece of curtain rail (Fig. 186 (a)). Attach a similar mass to a length of string and adjust the length so that it rises to the same height as the ball bearing (Fig. 186 (b)). When started at the same height which ball comes to rest first? Explain this in terms of energy transfer. Can you identify two types of kinetic energy in the rolling ball? Can you say how one type of kinetic energy is changed to the other in a flywheel-driven toy car?

Project 8.11. Can you make a double-cone run uphill? (Fig. 187). Explain what is happening.

Practical Puzzles

59. *A heavy trolley (M) is connected to a light trolley (m) by a stretched elastic thread (Fig. 188). They are released on a horizontal surface. Compared with the heavy one will the light one*

(a) *have a greater force acting on it at any time?*
(b) *gain more momentum before they collide?*
(c) *move further before they collide?*
(d) *reach a greater speed before they collide?*
(e) *have more kinetic energy before they collide?*

60. *Two heavy trolleys are joined by a stretched elastic thread. A needle is fixed to one trolley and a lump of plasticine to the other. When they are 1 metre apart on a horizontal surface they are released. The length of needle embedded in the plasticine is then measured. If the experiment is repeated under identical conditions with two very light trolleys, will the needle penetrate the plasticine by the same amount? Explain your answer (Fig. 189).*

Problems

61. *Find the kinetic energy of a hockey puck (mass = 0·17 kg) when it is travelling at 20 m/s.*
62. *What happens to the energy when work is done 'against' (a) gravity (b) inertia and (c) friction?*

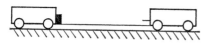

Fig. 189

63. *The ram of a piledriver has a mass of 50 kilograms. If it raised 5 metres above a post, find its potential energy. What will its velocity and kinetic energy just before it touches the post?*

64. *Find the energy required to increase the velocity of a sh (mass = 10^8 kg) from 5 m/s to 10 m/s.*

65. *Are the following statements true or false?*

(a) *A body can have mass and no weight.*
(b) *A body can have weight and no mass.*
(c) *Density depends on where a body is situated on the Eartk surface.*
(d) *The Earth has no weight.*
(e) *A rocket can propel itself in a vacuum.*
(f) *A lever increases your power.*
(g) *A grocer living on a hilltop uses a spring balance which w calibrated at sea-level. This is to the customer's advantage.*
(h) *Work is done whenever a force is exerted on something.*
(i) *All bodies fall at the same rate.*

66. *A car on a big dipper starts at A (Fig. 190). If there is friction, what will be its speed at B?*

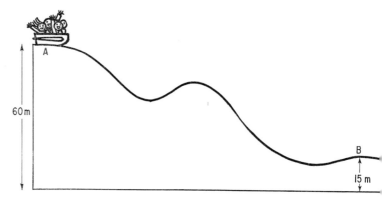

Fig. 190

67. *Why are road accidents at high speeds very much worse the accidents at low speeds?*

68. *Estimate the mass of a boy on a bicycle (in kilograms) and h speed (in metres per second) and hence estimate his kinetic energ (in joules).*

69. *Which of the following statements (if any) are correct? Whe the velocity of a moving body is doubled*

(a) *its acceleration is doubled,*
(b) *its momentum is doubled,*
(c) *its kinetic energy is doubled.*
(d) *its potential energy is doubled.*

70. *A man pushes a 40 kg box, originally at rest, along a horizont floor by exerting 113 newtons horizontally. The frictional for acting is 50 newtons.*

(a) *Find the unbalanced force.*
(b) *Find the acceleration of the box.*

(c) *Find the displacement of the box after moving for two seconds from rest.*
(d) *Find its speed after two seconds from rest.*
(e) *Find the energy supplied by the man in 2 seconds.*
(f) *Find the energy gained by the box.*
(g) *Find the energy lost as heat at the interface.*
(h) *Discuss the sum of (f) and (g).*

71. *A horizontal force of 36 N pushes a block P of mass 4 kg, which in turn pushes block Q of mass 5 kg, along a frictionless horizontal surface (Fig. 191).*

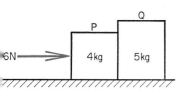

Fig. 191

(a) *What is the total mass accelerated?*
(b) *What is the acceleration produced?*
(c) *What is the horizontal force acting on Q?*
(d) *What exerts the force in (c)?*
(e) *What is the reaction to the force in (c)? State its magnitude and direction.*
(f) *What is the unbalanced force acting on P?*
(g) *If the blocks were at rest when the 36 N force was applied, calculate the kinetic energy of each block after 3 seconds.*
(h) *How far would they travel in that time?*
(i) *If the force was removed after 3 seconds, what would be the speed of Q after a further 3 seconds?*
(j) *If a frictional force of 4 N acted on the 4 kg block and 5 N on the 5 kg block, what unbalanced force would act on the two blocks if the applied force was still 36 N?*
Answer questions (a)–(i) again, assuming the friction stated in (j) acts. Letter these answers (k)–(s).

Collisions

Momentum (mass × velocity) is conserved in every collision. Is energy also conserved? To answer this question investigate the tapes you obtained from collisions with trolleys, or the strobe photographs of collisions with pucks or air track vehicles. Find the total kinetic energy before the collision and after the collision in each case.

Practical Puzzles

72. (a) *From Fig. 134, page 80, find the total kinetic energy of the vehicles before and after the collision. Assume each vehicle to have a mass of 1 unit and the flashes to be at 10 per second. Was kinetic energy conserved? If not what has happened to the energy? This is a completely inelastic collision.*

(b) *Repeat the above procedure for Fig. 135, page 81, remembering that this is an (almost) elastic collision. Was energy conserved? If you found that kinetic energy was conserved, can you explain why? If it was not conserved what happened to the energy?*

(c) *Can you find the total kinetic energy before and after the collision illustrated in Fig. 137, page 82?*

(d) *Find the kinetic energy of the bullet before striking the target in Demonstration 7.5 (a), page 82. What is the kinetic energy of the target plus bullet as they move off together? Explain your answer.*

From the answers to these questions you will have discovere
that kinetic energy is conserved in only one type of collision—a
elastic collision. In fact we can define an elastic collision as one i
which energy is conserved. All other collisions are inelastic and i
them energy is always transformed. *Into what forms may the energ
be changed?* (73)

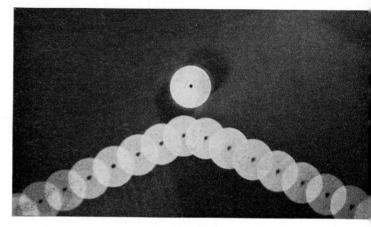

Fig. 192

Fig. 192 shows another example of an elastic collision. In thi
case a moving dry ice puck collides elastically with a stationary one
Compare the kinetic energy before and after the collision. (74) *Is th
momentum of the moving puck the same before and after the co.
lision?* (75) *Can you explain this?* (76) *Is kinetic energy conserve
as such, during the actual collision?* (77) *Explain.* (78)

Problems

79. *A truck of mass 10^4 kilograms is travelling at 4 m/s when i
collides with a stationary waggon (mass 5×10^4 kg). They ar
automatically coupled at impact and move off together.*

(a) *Find the momentum before and after the collision.*
(b) *Find the speed at which they move off.*
(c) *Find the total kinetic energy before and after impact. Explai
the result.*
(d) *Was this an elastic or an inelastic impact?*

80. (a) *Fig. 193 shows an elastic collision between two magnet
pucks of equal mass. Is the total kinetic energy the same before an
after the collision? What is the angle between the pucks as the
separate?*

(b) *Do you think kinetic energy is conserved in the collision illu
strated in Fig. 141 (page 84)? What kind of collision is this? I
kinetic energy a vector or scalar quantity?*

Collisions between particles

Molecules, atoms and atomic particles are continually collidin
with each other. The Wilson cloud chamber (Book 1, p. 54) wa
the first device which enabled physicists to study particle collision
Fig. 142 (page 85) shows a cloud chamber photograph of a collisio.

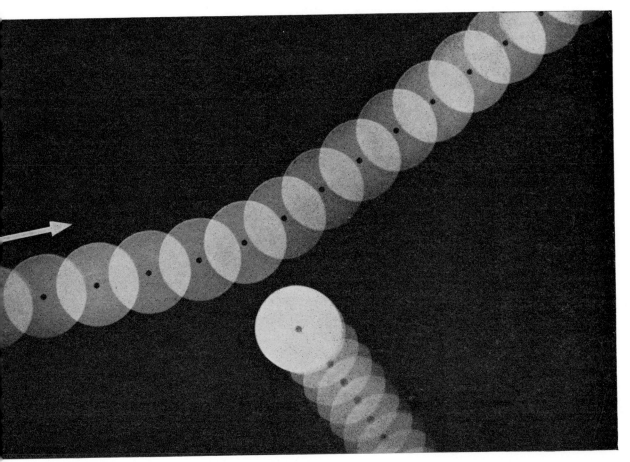

Fig. 193

between two particles. *Compare this with the magnetic puck collisions and, assuming atomic particles to behave similarly, state how you would interpret the cloud photograph.* (81)

Do you think that gas molecules will collide with the walls of their container elastically or inelastically? If inelastically what will happen (a) to the molecules after each collision and (b) to the energy transformed? (82)

Optional Extras

Efficiency of a Mini

The efficiency of a Mini can be calculated, assuming that a gallon of petrol can release 1.7×10^8 joules of energy, and that the car averages about 40 miles (64 km) per gallon at 40 miles per hour (18 m/s). We will find the energy used to keep the car (mass 750 kg) moving on a level road at about 40 miles per hour. First it is necessary to find the frictional forces at that speed. These forces can be estimated by finding how long it takes for the car to slow down on a level road from 50 miles per hour (22.5 m/s) to 30 miles

per hour (13·5 m/s) in neutral. A test indicated that it took 1
seconds for the car to slow down by (22·5 − 13·5) 9 m/s.

$$\text{Deceleration} = \frac{\text{change of velocity}}{\text{time}} = \frac{9}{15} \text{ m/s}^2$$

$$\text{Frictional forces} = m \times a = 750 \times \frac{9}{15} = 450 \text{ N}$$

$$\text{Work done in 1 hour} = F \times d = 450 \times 64000$$
$$= 2·88 \times 10^7 \text{ joules}$$

$$\text{Input of energy} = 1·7 \times 10^8 \text{ joules}$$

$$\text{Efficiency} \quad = \frac{2·88 \times 10^7}{17 \times 10^7} = 17 \text{ per cent}$$

The power of the engine during its hour's run can also be found.

$$\text{Power} = F \times v = 450 \times 18 = 8100 \text{ W}$$
$$= 8·1 \text{ kW}$$

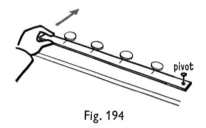

Fig. 194

Project 8.12. Project 4 pennies along a smooth horizontal surface
using a ruler pivoted at one end (Fig. 194). If they are spaced a
distances of 1, 2, 3 and 4 units from the pivot, they will be pro
jected with speeds of 1, 2, 3 and 4 units. How far do they travel
Can you discover an approximate connection between the distance
travelled and the speed of each penny? Explain this relationship
stating any assumptions you have to make.

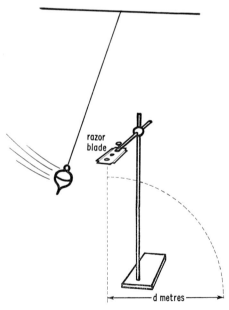

Fig. 195

Project 8.13. Can you devise an experiment to compare the
potential energy and maximum kinetic energy of a pendulum bob?

Here are some hints.

(*a*) Use a heavy bob and a ticker timer.

(*b*) Allow the bob to burst two narrow lengths of thin aluminium foil which are connected to a Panax scaler (see Demonstration 7.5 (*c*), page 82). If the tapes are a known distance apart the speed can then be found.

(*c*) Take a stroboscopic photograph of a pendulum and calculate the speed of the bob at its lowest point.

(*d*) Arrange a pendulum as shown in Fig. 195. When the bob reaches the bottom of its swing, cut or burn the thread and measure the distance *d*. How is *d* related to the maximum speed of the bob if it is released 1·25 metres above the ground? What assumptions have you made?

From your experiment what do you conclude?

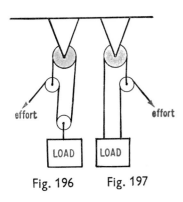

Fig. 196   Fig. 197

Project 8.14. Think about, then try, the pulley systems illustrated in Figs. 196 and 197. Comment on the results.

Project 8.15. Can you construct a puzzle box which runs *up* the string when you pull the lower string *down*? (Fig. 198).

Hint: The two strings run on to drums which resemble a machine you built in your first year.

Project 8.16. Set up the apparatus shown in Fig. 122 (page 72), and give the block a sharp push along a horizontal bench. Find the deceleration and hence the frictional force acting. Check your answer with a spring balance. Can you estimate the original kinetic energy of the block?

Project 8.17. Find the velocity ratio of a hand drill or egg beater.

Practical Puzzles

83. *A trolley, initially at rest, is pulled down a friction-compensated slope by a constant force. It pulls a ticker tape (Fig. 199) on which equal lengths are marked off from the starting point.*

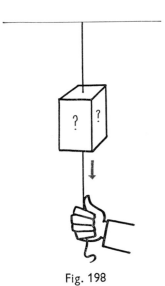

Fig. 198

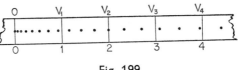

Fig. 199

How could the speeds at points v_1, v_2, v_3 and v_4 be estimated? How would these speeds be related to the lengths 1, 2, 3 and 4 units? Explain why there should be this relationship.

84. *A trolley is fired from an elastic band as shown in Fig. 200 and the speed is measured as the trolley runs along a friction-compensated slope. If the experiment were repeated using four identical elastic bands, each stretched by the same amount as before, how would the speed be affected?*

85. *Using the apparatus illustrated in Fig. 132 (page 80), find what percentage of the original kinetic energy of the trolley is changed to heat energy.*

86. *A ball bearing rolls down a slope and is then projected horizontally from the end. If it is released from a point 20 centimetres above the table, it strikes the floor d metres in front of the table*

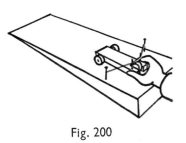

Fig. 200

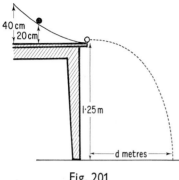

Fig. 201

Fig. 202

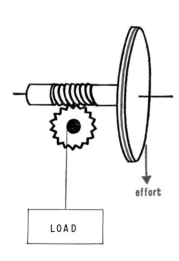

effort

LOAD

Fig. 203

(*Fig. 201*). *Approximately how far in front of the table would* *fall if it were released from a point 40 centimetres above the tabl* *Ignore frictional forces.*

87. *A trolley with spring-loaded plunger is placed at the end of* *friction-compensated runway. The end of the plunger is in conta* *with a heavy fixed body such as the end of the track. A ticker ta* *records the speed reached by the trolley after the 'explosion'. Let* *assume that the speed is v metres/second. If the experiment is r* *peated with two trolleys stacked on top of one another, or if the ma* *is doubled in some other way, will the speed reached this time* $\frac{v}{2}$, $2v$, $\frac{v}{\sqrt{2}}$, v? *Why?*

Additional Problems

88. *Can the man illustrated in Fig. 202 pull himself up?*

89. *Would the machine illustrated in Fig. 203 have a large or sma* *VR? Would its efficiency be high? Why?*

90. *A girl exerts a force of 10 newtons on the handle of an eg* *beater. If the circumference of the handle is 0·3 metres and she* *turning it three times a second, find her power in watts. What* *happening to this energy?*

91. *Find the power of a locomotive of mass 10^5 kg as it runs a* *10 m/s up a slope which rises by 2 m for every 100 m of rails, (a) ignor* *ing friction and (b) if the frictional forces are 3×10^3 newtons.*

92. *If a 60 kg man climbs a 600 m mountain, how much work i* *done? At 2d per kWh what would this amount of energy cost from* *the Electricity Board?*

93. *Find the air resistance on a jet p ane travelling at a constan* *speed of 200 m/s in level flight if the engine develops 2 megawatts* *Is the work done by the engine (a) directly proportional to tim* *(b) directly proportional to distance gone?*

94. *A train of mass 4×10^5 kilograms can free-wheel at a steady* *speed down an incline of 1 in 200. Find the frictional force opposing* *motion. If the frictional force remains the same, what wattage woul* *be used to drive the train at 20 m/s along a level track?*

95. *Will a car use more power if its tyres are hard or if they are* *soft? Why?*

96. *If a man runs up an upward moving escalator at a constan* *speed will the motor have to do more work? Explain.*

97. *Find the kinetic energy of (a) a cricket ball of mass 170 g* *travelling at 30 m/s and (b) an electron of mass 9×10^{-31} kg shooting* *through a television tube at 3×10^7 m/s.*

98. *During a fog two cars run into a wall. Police find the damage* *done is about the same in each case and take statements from the* *drivers. One driver claims to have been doing 40 mi/h and the other* *in a car of four times the mass claims to have been travelling at only* *10 mi/h. Do you think both drivers were honest? Explain the con-* *clusion you reach.*

99. *A trolley fitted with a needle runs into a large fixed block of* *plasticine. The needle penetrates 1 inch. If another trolley fitted* *with an identical needle were fired with twice the momentum at a* *similar block of plasticine, would the needle penetrate 1 inch, more* *than 1 inch, less than 1 inch or can you not say? Explain the answer* *you give.*

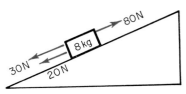

Fig. 204

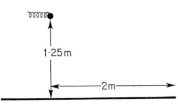

1·25 m

—2m—

Fig. 205

100. *A box of mass 8 kilograms is pulled up a slope by a force of 80 newtons (Fig. 204). If the gravitational force acting down the slope is 30 newtons and the frictional force 20 newtons, find*

(a) *the unbalanced force acting on the box,*
(b) *its acceleration up the slope,*
(c) *its kinetic energy after travelling for 5 metres,*
(d) *the potential energy gained,*
(e) *the energy transformed to heat by friction,*
(f) *the sum of (c), (d) and (e),*
(g) *the work done by the applied force.*

101. *A ball of mass 0·04 kg is projected horizontally by a compressed spring. When released the ball is in contact with the spring as it moves forward 0·02 m. The ball is released from a height of 1·25 m and falls 2 m in front of the release point (Fig. 205).*
Taking g as 10 m/s² and ignoring air resistance, find

(a) *the time taken for the ball to fall,*
(b) *the velocity of the ball when it leaves the spring,*
(c) *the velocity of the ball just before it lands,*
(d) *the momentum of the ball as it leaves the spring,*
(e) *the impulse on the ball,*
(f) *the (average) acceleration of the ball while being pushed by the spring,*
(g) *the average force acting on the ball as it accelerates,*
(h) *the time during which the ball is accelerated horizontally,*
(i) *the KE of the ball as it leaves the spring,*
(j) *the PE of the ball as it leaves the spring,*
(k) *the KE of the ball just before it touches the ground,*
(l) *the PE of the ball just before it touchss the ground.*

102. *A hammer head (mass 0·6 kg) is travelling at 4 metres per second just before it strikes a nail. If the nail (of negligible mass) is driven 2 centimetres into a piece of wood, find the kinetic energy of the hammer head and hence the average resistance. Can you find the resistive force by another method?*

103. *A bullet of mass 0·02 kilograms is fired horizontally into a sandbag of mass 7·98 kilograms. The sandbag is suspended as a pendulum and is seen to rise 0·08 metres (measured vertically). If the bullet remains embedded in the sandbag,*

(a) *find the speed of the bullet,*
(b) *find the kinetic energy before and after impact,*
(c) *how do you explain the results you obtain?*
(d) *what percentage of the original mechanical energy remained in this form after the impact?*

104. *In a particle accelerator 3×10^4 protons are accelerated from rest to 2×10^7 metres/second in one second. If each particle has a mass of $1·7 \times 10^{-27}$ kg, find the total kinetic energy of the particles.*

105. *Einstein's equation $E = mc^2$ gives the energy equivalent (in joules) locked up in m kilograms of matter. If the velocity of light (c) is taken as 3×10^8 m/s, find the energy equivalent of 1 gram of matter. How much would this amount of energy cost from the Electricity Board if it charges 2d per kWh?*

106. *If the Mini used in the example on page 113 can accelerate uniformly from 13·5 m/s to 22·5 m/s in 10 seconds, find*

(a) *its acceleration,*
(b) *the unbalanced force needed to cause this acceleration,*
(c) *the total force exerted on the car (assuming frictional forces as before),*
(d) *the average speed during acceleration,*
(e) *the power of the car during acceleration,*
(f) *the kinetic energy of the car at 13·5 m/s (30 mi/h) and at 22·5 m/s (50 mi/h).*

107. *A car of mass 10^3 kg is travelling at 10 m/s on a horizontal road. It then accelerates to 20 m/s in 15 seconds.*

(a) *Find the acceleration of the car.*
(b) *Find the accelerating force—assumed to be constant.*
(c) *Find the kinetic energy of the car before acceleration.*
(d) *Find the kinetic energy of the car after acceleration.*
(e) *Find the work done in accelerating the car.*
(f) *Find the power of the engine in watts during acceleration.*
(g) *By equating the work done to accelerate the car with the unbalanced force multiplied by distance, find the distance gone during acceleration.*

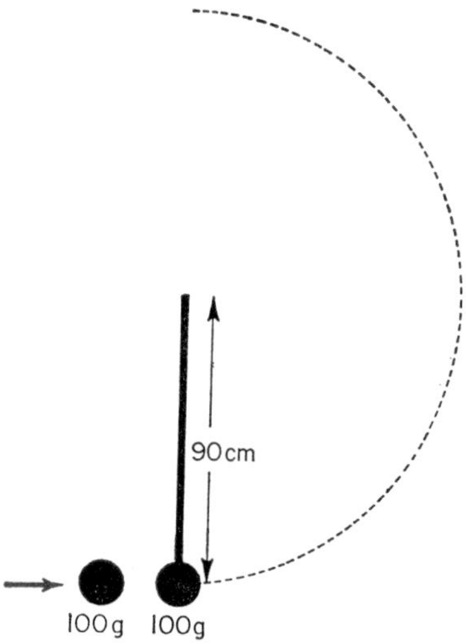

108. *A car of mass 10^3 kilograms travelling at 10 metres per second is brought to rest in 20 metres. Find*

(a) *the original kinetic energy of the vehicle,*
(b) *the final kinetic energy of the vehicle,*
(c) *the heat energy produced by the brakes,*
(d) *the work done by force F in stopping the car,*
(e) *the force F by equating (c) and (d),*
(f) *the force F by another method.*

109. *A 100 gram steel ball is attached to a 90 centimetre rod. The rod can be assumed to be weightless and rigid, and pivoted as shown in Fig. 206. A second identical steel ball is projected horizontally so that it collides elastically with the first. What must be the speed if the second is to revolve round the pivot? To solve this question answer the following.*

(a) *What would be the maximum potential energy gained by the second ball when it was at the top of its circular path?*
(b) *What must be the minimum kinetic energy with which it starts off?*
(c) *What must be the kinetic energy of the free ball just before the collision?*
(d) *What is the speed of the free ball?*

110. *A heavy metal block is suspended from a coil spring (Fig. 207). The clamp holding the spring is adjusted so that when the block is released from position A (spring unstretched) it stops, just before touching the base at position C. The gravitational potential energy at C is taken as zero. How would you find (a) the gravitational potential energy at A, (b) the elastic potential energy at C and (c) the kinetic energy at B?*

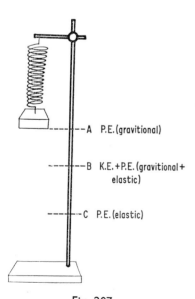

90 cm

100 g   100 g

Fig. 206

A   P.E. (gravitional)

B   K.E. + P.E. (gravitional + elastic)

C   P.E. (elastic)

Fig. 207

Visual Aids

Filmstrips: Energy and Man. Force and Energy$_{22}$ S10.
Energy and Man. Mechanical Energy$_{22}$ S11.
16 mm Films: Energy and its transformations$_{23}$ 20.7344.
Simple Machines$_{23}$ 20.3872.
Energy and Work$_{23}$ 21.7484.
Energy and Work (P.S.S.C.)$_{26}$ 3D.2715.
Elastic Collisions and Stored Energy (P.S.S.C.)$_{26}$.

Heat and Hot

CHAPTER 9

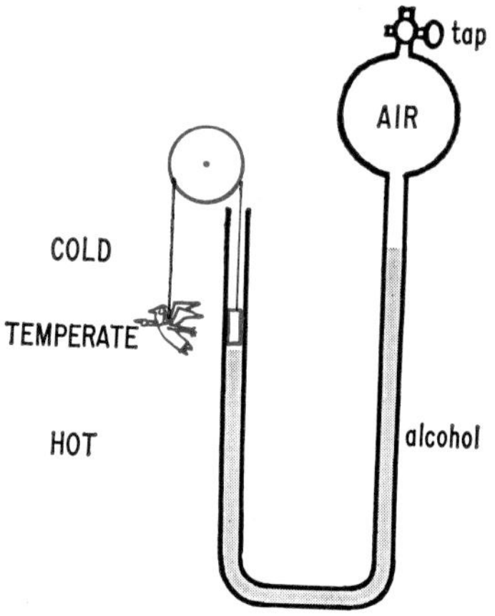

Angels on Alcohol

Before continuing your study of heat and temperature you should revise Book 1, chapter 10, and make sure that you can answer all the questions asked in that chapter.

Although notions of 'hot' and 'cold' are inbred in man, it was not until 1592 that the first instrument for measuring temperature was invented. This was Galileo's air thermometer or thermoscope. *Why was it not entirely satisfactory?* (1) Otto von Guericke later constructed an improved version in which alcohol in a U-tube was used to enclose the air. A float on the surface of the liquid in the open arm rose and fell as the volume of air in the bulb varied. A little angel was tied to a cord which passed over a pulley and was then attached to the float (Fig. 208). The angel indicated whether it was hot, temperate, or cold. The thermometer was supposed to be calibrated on a summer's evening, just before harvest, when the temperature was moderate! Air was then drawn out of, or pumped into, the globe until the angel was in the 'temperate' position.

Does this thermometer overcome the snags of Galileo's thermoscope? (2)

Fig. 208

Fixed Points

The evolution of the thermometer was a slow process, and it was not until more than 100 years after Galileo's original invention that a temperature scale was devised. During that hundred years many modifications took place. In 1631 Ray used the expansion of water in a bulb as shown in Fig. 209. *What disadvantages can you find in this arrangement?* (3) Later, alcohol was used, as it freezes at a much lower temperature than water, and the top of the tube was sealed. *Can you suggest reasons for doing this?* (4)

The next step was to use mercury. Although its expansion is much less than that of alcohol, mercury can be used in very narrow tubes as it is easily seen. The mercury was cleaned by filtering it through leather. In later thermometers the space above the liquid was evacuated. *What difference would this make?* (5)

All the early thermometers had one major defect; they did not have a common scale. It was left to the user to interpret the markings on the thermometer as he felt inclined! These uncalibrated thermometers were, however, used to make some important discoveries, among them the fact that under normal conditions water always freezes at the same temperature, and always boils at the same temperature.

In 1665 Boyle suggested that the freezing point of water might be used as a 'fixed point', and in 1693 Halley suggested the boiling

Fig. 209

point of water as a 'fixed point'. It seems incredible that for years no one thought of using these two fixed points to construct a scale of temperature, and when in 1724 the German physicist, Gabriel Daniel Fahrenheit, set up the first acceptable temperature scale, he used two other much less reliable fixed points. He obtained the lowest temperature then known, by mixing water, ice, and sal ammoniac. This temperature he called 0° on his mercury thermometer. His upper fixed point was 96°—the temperature of the 'normal' human body.

Why, you may wonder, did Fahrenheit choose 96 degrees? In 1701 Sir Isaac Newton proposed a scale of temperatures in which the lower fixed point was the freezing point of water, and the upper fixed point was the temperature of the human body. This he divided into 12 degrees. *Can you list some other instances of things which are divided into twelve parts?* (6) *Can you think of a possible origin of the use of this number?* (7)

Fahrenheit decided to use the lowest temperature he could obtain for the zero of his scale. Like Newton he took body temperature as the upper fixed point, and divided the interval into twelve equal parts. To obtain finer graduations each of these was further subdivided into eight equal parts, making a range of 96 degrees all of equal size. Later Fahrenheit extended his scale using degrees of the same size. On this scale the freezing point of water was 32 degrees and the boiling point of water 212 degrees.

In 1730 Réaumur devised a scale which had 80 equal divisions between the freezing and boiling points of water, and in 1742 Anders Celsius, a Swedish astronomer, suggested a scale of 100 divisions between the same fixed points. It is the Celsius, or Centigrade, scale which we use today.

The Right Temperature

One of Lewis Carroll's characters had a watch which was always 'right' because it controlled the passing of time. If the watch went fast time speeded up as well. The measurement of temperature is 'controlled' by a thermometer in the sense that once a scale on a mercury thermometer has been marked off in equal degrees, *temperature is defined*. It was soon found that when liquids other than mercury were used in thermometers the scales did not correspond exactly at every temperature. The mercury scale was taken as the standard.

Later it was discovered that when gases were used in thermometers the various gas scales agreed with each other more closely than the scales of liquid thermometers. You might like to construct a simple gas thermometer. In it you should keep the volume of the gas constant (or very nearly) and measure the change in pressure with temperature.

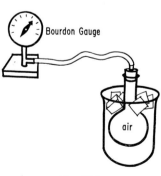

Bourdon Gauge

air

Fig. 210

Experiment 9.1. (*a*) Connect a 100 cm³ flask to a Bourdon pressure gauge₃ which is calibrated in absolute units of pressure (Fig. 210). Note the pressure when the flask is immersed in boiling water (100°C), a mixture of ice and water (0°C), and a mixture of dry ice and methylated spirits (−72°C). Construct a graph showing how the pressure varies with the temperature. At what temperature would the pressure of the air be zero?

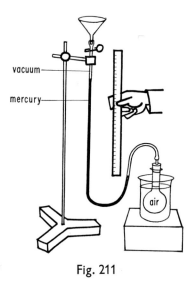

Fig. 211

Use this apparatus as a thermometer to find the temperature of (say) warm water, and check your result with a mercury thermometer.

(b) An alternative and more direct method of measuring the pressure is to use a length of transparent Vinyl tubing₁₂ (Portland N.T.5) filled with mercury (Fig. 211). Use a small plastic funnel₃ to fill the tube, and then clamp it when the open limb is full of mercury. In this way a simple mercury barometer can be constructed. It will measure directly the absolute pressure of the gas in the flask. Measure the pressure of the gas at various temperatures and plot a graph of your results. Can you mark off a scale of temperature on the metre stick? What would zero pressure indicate?

Use this gas thermometer, once calibrated, to measure water at an unknown temperature. Compare this reading with the reading on a mercury thermometer.

The temperature at which the pressure of a gas would disappear —if it continued to decrease uniformly—is called *absolute zero*. It is about 273 Celsius (or Centigrade) degrees below the freezing point of water. At Oxford recently Professor Kurti has obtained temperatures in the neighbourhood of a millionth of a degree above absolute zero.

In 1852 Lord Kelvin established a new and quite different scale of temperature. It was no longer dependent on the expansion or change of pressure of a particular substance. This new theoretical scale, which we will not attempt to describe here, is called the thermodynamic scale. The size of the degrees on the thermodynamic scale is the same as those on the Celsius scale, but absolute zero is taken as 0°K, that is, −273·15° Celsius = 0° Kelvin.

For our purposes we will take

$$0°K = -273°C$$
$$273°K = 0°C$$
$$373°K = 100°C$$

Temperatures in the universe are thought to range from very near absolute zero in outer space to perhaps thousands of millions of degrees Kelvin at the centre of an exploding star.

The choice of mercury for use in the original standard thermometers turned out to be a very fortunate one, as the readings agree with the thermodynamic scale to within a fraction of a degree over most of the range.

Thermocouples

You have already constructed a simple thermocouple and used it to test the hottest part of a bunsen flame. Thermocouples are extremely sensitive instruments and they take very little heat from the substance they are measuring. Delicate thermocouples fitted inside astronomical telescopes can be used to measure the temperature of a planet. Later in the course we will be using the meter₁₄ (Galvo-amplifier) illustrated in Fig. 212 in conjunction with a copper/constantan thermocouple to indicate small temperature changes. You might like to use such an instrument now to detect infra-red radiation from your hand placed close to the thermo-couple.

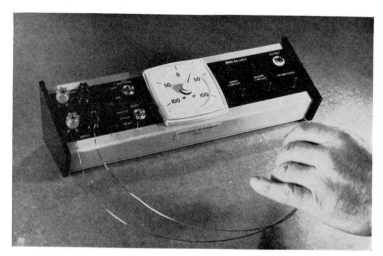

Fig. 212

Practical Puzzles

8. *Using the apparatus illustrated in Fig. 212 dip the thermocouple into methylated spirit. Note the meter reading. Now remove the thermocouple from the liquid and explain the new reading. When you take the thermocouple out of the methylated spirit is it reading the temperature of the air in the room?*

9. *Paint the bulb of one mercury thermometer white, and the bulb of another black. Do the two thermometers read the same when they are near an electric radiator? Explain the readings you obtain.*

Problem 10. *Two thermometers, one filled with mercury and one with water, are used side by side. It is found that the water thermometer gives the same reading at two different temperature readings on the mercury thermometer. Can you explain why this could happen?*

Measuring Heat

Once a reliable temperature scale had been devised, the stage was set to investigate the relationship between temperature and heat. Until then the two concepts had not been clearly distinguished. The Scots scientist, Joseph Black (1728–1799), seems to have been the first man to think of heat as a definite physical quantity which could be measured. In the following experiments you can find out one way of doing this.

Experiment 9.2. You can assume that a 12 volt immersion heater$_{3.9}$ supplies heat at a steady rate, so that in 2 minutes it will supply twice as much heat as in 1 minute. By using an Aerocup$_4$ made of expanded polystyrene (an excellent heat insulator), you may ignore any heat absorbed by the cup or lost to the atmosphere during the experiment.

Pour about 0·15 kg of water into the cup and insert the immersion heater as shown in Fig. 213. Read the original temperature of the

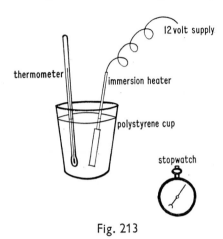

thermometer

immersion heater

polystyrene cup

12 volt supply

stopwatch

Fig. 213

water to 1 place of decimals, using a lens if necessary, and switch on the heater for 30 seconds. Stir the water with the immersion heater and read the maximum temperature obtained. Calculate the increase in temperature.

Now switch the heater on for another 30 seconds, read the final temperature, and again calculate the temperature change *from the original water temperature*. Repeat this procedure several times and complete the following table.

Plot a graph showing the temperature change against heat supplied. What does the graph suggest?

Time in seconds—proportional to heat supplied (ΔH)	30	60	90	120	150
Increase in temperature from start of heating (ΔT)					

Experiment 9.3. (*a*) Using the same apparatus as before pour 0·1 kg of cold water into the cup and note how long it takes to raise the temperature by (say) 5°C. Stir the water during this time. Repeat the experiment with 0·2 kg and 0·3 kg of water contained in a small polystyrene flowerpot.

Time in seconds (ΔH)			
Mass of water in kilograms (m)	0·1	0·2	0·3

(b) Alternatively you can use larger polystyrene flowerpots in conjunction with a 300 watt mains-operated immersion heater and larger masses of water.

The results of the above experiments indicate that the heat supplied is proportional to the *change* of temperature if the mass is constant, and to the mass if the temperature change is constant. For the moment we will use an old heat unit, the *calorie*, or rather its big brother the *kilocalorie*. The kilocalorie is sometimes called the Big Calorie or simply the Calorie written with a capital C. The kilocalorie is the heat needed to raise the temperature of 1 kilogram of water by 1 degree centigrade.

Remembering the results of the last two experiments, complete the following table.

To raise temp. of 1 kg of water by 1°C the heat needed is 1 kcal.

To raise temp. of 20 kg of water by 1°C the heat needed is   kcal.

To raise temp. of *m* kg of water by 1°C the heat needed is   kcal.

To raise temp. of *m* kg of water by 5°C the heat needed is   kcal.

To raise temp. of *m* kg of water by ΔT°C the heat needed is   kcal.

Here then is a simple way of measuring the heat supplied to water.

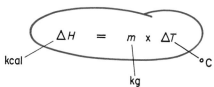

Is Heat Conserved?

In the next experiment you should use the relationship you have just found to see if heat is conserved.

Experiment 9.4. Pour some cold water into one Aerocup and some hot water into another. Note the masses and the temperatures. Now pour the contents of the cups into a third cup, stir the mixture and read the new temperature immediately. Call it x°C. Calculate the heat lost by the hot water and the heat gained by the cold. Are they the same?

Using the quantities shown in Fig. 214 we would have

$$\text{Heat lost by the hot water} = m.\Delta T$$
$$= 0\cdot 1 \,(60 - x) \text{ kcal.}$$

$$\text{Heat gained by the cold water} = m.\Delta T$$
$$= 0\cdot 05 \,(x - 20) \text{ kcal.}$$

What does this experiment tell you? Do you think this is a general rule?

Try a similar experiment using two mugs or copper calorimeters and see if you get the same results. Can you explain any differences?

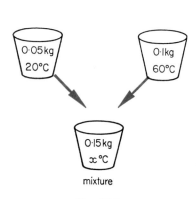

Fig. 214

Are All Materials Alike?

So far we have measured heat by measuring the temperature rise of a mass of water. *Can we use the same technique for other substances?* (11)

Experiment 9.5. Using the same method as used in Experiment 9.4 add (say) 0·08 kg of water at 60°C to 0·08 kg of water at room temperature and note the mixture temperatures.

Now take another Aerocup containing 0·08 kg of water at 60°C and add to it 0·08 kg of copper rivets at room temperature. Stir the mixture with a glass rod (*not* a thermometer) and find the final temperatures.

Were the two final temperatures the same? Is the heat gained by the copper expressed by $m \times \Delta T$? Think about these questions: we will return to them later.

Visual Aids

Filmstrips: Energy and Man. Heat Energy[22] S12, S13, S15.
16 mm Films: Heat: Its nature and transfer[23] 20.7222.
What's in a Flame[27]?

Thermodynamics

CHAPTER 10

What is Heat?

Living in the 20th century, when electricity can supply us with mechanical energy, heat, light and sound it is not difficult for us to appreciate that there must be something common to all these things. It is, of course, energy. It is well to remember, however, that not much more than 100 years ago this was not obvious, even to some of the most brilliant men of the time. In this chapter we will trace the search for an understanding of heat and look briefly at some of the ideas put forward.

It is relatively easy to select from history only those ideas which are seen today to have been 'ahead of their time'. It must be remembered, however, that other ideas about heat were suggested and that many of these have long since been shown to be inadequate. We will consider briefly one of these, the caloric theory, but in general we will select only the ideas which have borne fruit.

More than 2,000 years ago Plato asserted that heat is 'begotten by impact and friction . . . but this is *motion*'. In the 17th century Francis Bacon said that 'heat is motion and nothing else'. We might add that he listed mustard as 'hot' and moonbeams as 'cold'! At the end of the 17th century Huygens said that flame and fire must contain particles in rapid motion for they 'melt the most solid substances', and a few years later John Locke claimed that heat is a 'very brisk agitation of the insensible parts of the object'. About the turn of the century, Leibnitz, the German mathematician and philosopher, suggested that when inelastic bodies collide the energy is not lost but 'dissipated among the minute parts' of the bodies.

During the 18th century Robert Hooke said that heat is 'nothing else other than a brisk and vehement agitation of the parts of a body', and Robert Boyle explained the heating of a nail when struck by a hammer by saying that the hammer 'impresses a vehement agitation on the small parts of the iron'. In the same century Daniel Bernoulli explained the pressure of a gas in terms of the impacts of flying molecules on the walls of the container. Towards the end of the 18th century Lavoisier and Laplace gave the mechanical theory their blessing, and said that as each moving particle in a substance had kinetic energy, *heat* was the sum of the kinetic energies of all the particles in the substance.

In spite of the strong body of opinion in favour of the mechanical theory of heat (heat is the movement of the particles of a body) it must be admitted that it was just opinion. There was little direct experimental evidence to support the theory, and consequently there grew up during the 18th century a rival theory which gained increasing support as it seemed to explain most heat phenomena.

The Discarded Model

Dr Cleghorn's caloric theory (1779) described heat as an elastic fluid, which could pass from one substance to another. A hot substance contained more caloric than a cold substance, and so caloric always flowed from hot to cold. The particles of caloric were attracted by ordinary matter but repelled each other and they could neither be created nor destroyed. As new discoveries were made the theory altered to suit the experimental results. When it was discovered that the temperature did not change when boiling water changed to steam, two types of caloric were suggested: sensible caloric, which raised the temperature of a body and latent (hidden) caloric, which combined with the particles of a body to form a new substance. There was some argument as to whether or not caloric had mass and so it was claimed that it might or might not have mass. Lavoisier suggested that caloric might be a chemical element.

The caloric theory gave a reasonable explanation for many heat phenomena. Heat does 'flow' from a hot to a cold body. This was because the greater number of particles in the hot body repelled each other and were forced into the cold body. Heat produced by friction was explained by saying that when rubbed a body lost some of its 'capacity for heat.' Thermal expansion was due to the caloric forcing its way into a substance and conduction of heat resulted from the particles of caloric repelling each other.

There seemed little doubt that for most practical purposes the caloric model of heat provided an adequate explanation, and it was accepted by many of the leading scientists of the day. Even today we still speak of 'heat flow' as if it were a fluid and 'heat capacity', which tends to suggest that a body can hold a certain amount of fluid. The unit of heat, the calorie, still being used in some quarters, also reminds us of the caloric theory.

We do not ask, 'Is this theory true?' but rather, 'Does it fit all the experimental facts and enable us to make correct predictions?'. By the end of the 18th century there were many people who claimed that it did not measure up to these requirements. The next advance was made not by theoretical scientists but by practical men, most of whom were young men who were not professional physicists when they made their discoveries.

The Amateur Physicists

Benjamin Thomson (Count Rumford) *1753–1814*

The next phase of the story began in the 18th century and reached its climax during the first half of the 19th century. It began with one of the most amazing men in the history of science, yet one who is all but forgotten: Benjamin Thomson. An excellent biography of Thomson by Professor Sanborn C. Brown is aptly entitled 'Count Rumford: Physicist Extraordinary'. Born in the middle of the 18th century in America, Thomson, as he supported the Tories in the War of Independence, had to flee to Britain, where he soon became Under Secretary of State in the Ministry for the Colonies. By the age of 26 he was a Fellow of the Royal Society. He became a

Colonel in the British Army and was knighted by George III. He left England and became Minister of War in Bavaria where he was made a Count of the Holy Roman Empire. Later he returned to England, formed the Royal Institution in 1799, and spent the last years of his life in France, where he married the widow of the famous chemist, Antoine Lavoisier.

Professor Brown suggests that his ruthless egotism and violent overbearing manner are perhaps the main reasons for Rumford's obscurity. Many of his acquaintances who might have kept his memory alive tried to forget him as soon as possible. When he was in his forties he is on record as boasting, 'I never was yet in the wrong. I know everything'. Towards the end of his life he became extremely eccentric and could be seen walking the streets of Paris in shiny white clothes, which he believed reflected cold 'frigorific' rays, which if absorbed would cool him down! *Can you think how you might investigate whether or not such cold rays exist?* (1)

Count Rumford's inventions are too numerous to list in full but they included photometers, fireplaces, lamps, steam heating systems and coffee makers. He was responsible for the design of new kitchen equipment and many improvements in the washing house and dining hall of George Heriot's School in Edinburgh. For this he was presented with a silver snuff box!

It is, however, for his attacks on the caloric theory and his experiments to disprove it, that Rumford is remembered. He took great pains to weigh three flasks of water, mercury and alcohol before and after heating them. He discovered no detectable increase in the weight, and concluded that if caloric existed it was so rare that one calorie could weigh no more than 10^{-8} grams. Einstein showed later that the mass equivalent of one calorie is actually about a millionth of this!

Most people know only one thing about Rumford—he bored cannons! While he was Inspector General of the Artillery for the Bavarian army he was responsible for the production of military guns and cannon. In the arsenal of Munich he adapted cannon-boring machines to enable him to conduct heat experiments. In one experiment he used a blunt borer, which produced so much heat that he was able to boil two and a half gallons of water, much to the entertainment of the local population. He wrote, 'It is difficult to describe the astonishment on the countenances of the bystanders on seeing so large a quantity of cold water heated and actually made to boil without any fire'. Rumford also showed that the heat capacity of the cannon borer and metal shavings were the same before and after the drilling process. Rumford's claim was that the amount of heat which could be produced by friction was inexhaustible and therefore could not be explained by the caloric theory. The heat, he said, was coming from the work done by the horses and ultimately by the oxidation of the fodder they had eaten. He used the following analogy to present his arguments against the calorists. If you continue squeezing a wet sponge you cannot get water from it for ever (caloric theory), but a ringing bell will continue to produce sound as long as it is struck (mechanical theory). He said of his cannon-boring experiments, 'It appears to me to be extremely difficult, if not quite impossible, to form any distinct ideas of anything capable of being excited and communicated in

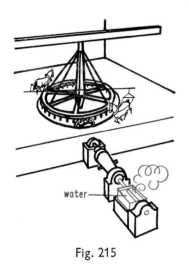

water

Fig. 215

the manner the heat was excited and communicated in these experiments except it be *motion*!'

Rumford's results were not given the kind of welcome he had hoped for: folk don't like to give up their old ideas. Fifty years later the *Encyclopaedia Britannica* was still giving preference to the caloric theory!

There is no evidence to suggest that Rumford ever attempted to measure the work his horses did or the heat produced. He was content to show that mechanical work could produce a *limitless amount of heat*. He never suggested that heat and work were two aspects of the same thing, that is, that energy is conserved. The foundations had, however, been laid, and the first half of the 19th century produced the necessary evidence from a variety of sources. We will consider only a few.

Julius Robert Mayer (*1814–1878*)

Mayer, a young German doctor, was on a voyage to Java when he noticed that the blood from the veins of his patients was a much brighter red than that in the veins of his patients in Germany. Mayer knew that the body's heat is produced by oxidation, and he explained his observation by saying that the body needs to produce less heat in a hot climate and therefore there is less oxidation of the sugars in the blood. Mayer then reasoned that the oxidation produces

(a) heat which is lost to the atmosphere as the body temperature is higher than the atmospheric temperature, and
(b) mechanical work which can in turn heat the atmosphere, for example, by friction.

He then said that in both cases the heat produced was proportional to the oxygen consumed, and so the mechanical work, before it is changed to heat, must also be proportional to the oxygen consumed. Mayer concluded that heat and work must be equivalent and that it should be possible to change heat into work or work into heat *at a fixed rate of exchange*. Mayer knew very little physics and he had no real evidence to back up his theory but he returned home and devoted all his time and energy to an intensive study of the subject. One story relates a visit to the physicist, Jolly, at the end of which Jolly remarked in jest that if Mayer's theory was true it should be possible to heat water merely by shaking it. Many weeks later a figure entered Jolly's room shouting, 'It is so!'. So convinced was Mayer that work, chemical energy, heat, light, electricity and magnetism were all forms of energy and that a fixed amount of mechanical energy was *exactly* equivalent to a certain quantity of heat that he produced several papers, all of which were laughed at by most of the physicists of the day. He became so depressed that in 1850 he attempted to commit suicide by throwing himself out of a window. Although not killed he was physically and mentally handicapped for the remainder of his life. He had arrived at the correct answer, that there is a mechanical equivalent of heat, but it was rejected for many years because he could not justify his theory either by accurate experiment or by convincing argument. (Or was it just plain pig-headedness on the part of the scientists?)

Fortunately Mayer did live to see his theory generally accepted. In 1854 Helmholtz recognised Mayer's work and in 1871 Mayer was presented with the Royal Society's highest honour, the Copley Medal.

James Prescott Joule (*1818–1898*)

The Manchester brewer, James Prescott Joule, worked during the same period as Mayer. Like Mayer he was not a professional physicist and both came to the same conclusion. There, however, the similarity ends. In place of the vague pseudo-scientific evidence of Mayer, Joule presented the results of forty years of painstaking precision. During that time he had devised, built and used the most elaborate and accurate equipment ever designed to investigate the relationship between mechanical work and heat. If Mayer is given credit for stating the theory, Joule must be honoured as the man who showed it to work in practice.

When he was 19 Joule built an electric motor and measured the input and output of energy. He was anxious to see if such a machine could replace a steam engine. To his disappointment he discovered that a pound of zinc in the battery allowed the electric motor to do the same amount of work as a fifth of a pound of coal in a steam engine!

Joule then built an electric generator and discovered that electric current produced heat when he turned the handle. Could this heat be measured? Joule decided to immerse the dynamo coil in water

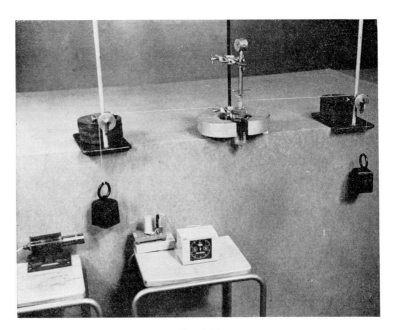

Fig. 216

and note the change of temperature. Fig. 216 shows a Heath-Robinson attempt to reconstruct Joule's experiment. Here, however, modern materials and methods are being used.

Project 10.1. This is the kind of project you might like to try for an open day or science club. You must first do some research on your own and then use your ingenuity to construct a model which will work. In the model illustrated, 'weights' were added to the strings until they fell at a steady speed, which was measured (Fig. 216). From this information the mechanical power input was calculated. The rate of turning of the armature was then found, and the experiment was repeated using an electric drill to turn the armature at the same rate for a much longer time. Don't expect the same results as Joule obtained: remember that he devoted his life to this kind of work!

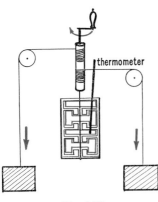

Fig. 217

Having found that the same amount of heat was always produced, electrically, from the same amount of mechanical energy, Joule thought it should be possible to convert mechanical energy into heat *directly* without the intermediary of the electric current. He tried various methods including forcing water through very small tubes but he eventually decided on the famous paddle-wheel (Fig. 217).

He used the same technique as before to measure the mechanical energy put in, and measured the temperature of the water before and after churning. If you think this is an easy experiment—try it! One school group discovered that the temperature *fell* after churning. *Can you explain that?* (2)

One of Joule's original paddle wheels is now in the Science Museum at South Kensington, and you can see a model in Joule House, Acton Street, Salford.

Joule's enthusiasm for his work was such that he took a thermometer with him on his honeymoon to Switzerland! Lord Kelvin reports finding him during that holiday measuring the temperature of the water at the top and the bottom of a long waterfall (Fig. 218). *Would you expect the temperature to be higher at the top or the bottom?* (3) *Why?* (4)

Fig. 218

In his experiments Joule used electric motors, dynamos and paddle wheels. He also investigated the compression of gases, and the loss of potential energy when a body falls under gravity. In every case he was convinced that there was the *same* relationship between the mechanical work done and the heat produced. So exact were his measurements that one might have expected that the scientists of the day would have accepted them. This was not so. It took many years of continuous persuasion and presentation of results before a few people started to take notice. It was said of Joule that scientists would not believe him because he had 'nothing but hundredths of a degree to prove his case by'. When the Royal Society refused to publish one of his papers he did not jump out of a window: his sense of humour saved him. He said that he could imagine the London gentlemen sitting round a table and saying, 'What good can come out of a town (Manchester) where they dine in the middle of the day!' Being able to give this reply could be more important than being able to verify the first law of thermodynamics!

It was not until 30 years after his first reported experiments that the Royal Society awarded Joule the Copley Medal. This they did one year before giving it to Mayer.

How and Why?

Joule answered the question, '*How* does mechanical energy change into heat?' by asserting that the exchange rate was fixed. One unit of work always changed into the same amount of heat. He did not claim that motion by itself produced heat, only that heat was produced when the motion was arrested. He always measured the work done against some frictional force. His reply to the *why* question was a theological one. 'It is absurd,' he claimed, 'to suppose that the energy with which God has endowed matter can be destroyed'.

Hirn, a French engineer, found a value similar to Joule's for the mechanical equivalent of heat when he caused lumps of metal to collide inelastically. In the following experiment you can see that heat is produced on impact when a hammer strikes a piece of lead.

lead

Fig. 219

Experiment 10.2. Insert a small thermocouple between two small pieces of lead sheet as shown in Fig. 219. Strike the lead with a hammer and note the result produced.

Conversion Factor

In the next two experiments we will attempt to arrive at a rough estimation of the conversion factor between work in newton metres (joules) and heat in kilocalories.

Experiment 10.3. Take the copper cylinder from a Cottingham J apparatus$_4$ and find how much heat is required to raise its temperature by 1°C. This amount of heat is called the *heat capacity*. Can you think of a simple way to do this using an Aerocup and some warm water?

An alternative method of finding the heat capacity of the cylinder uses a small electric heater of about 4 ohms. It can be calibrated by placing it in water and measuring the temperature rise when (say) 3 amperes flow for a known time.

Make sure that the cylinder is thoroughly dry and fix it between two felt pads. Pour a drop of oil into the hole and insert a thermometer. What is the oil for? Note the temperature before and after pulling the string a known distance (*d* metres) under constant tension (*F* newtons) as shown in Fig. 220.

As you know the heat required to raise the temperature of the cylinder 1°C you can calculate the heat developed during the experiment. How many joules are equivalent to one kilocalorie?

Heat needed to raise the temp. of the cylinder by 1°C =   kcal

Temperature rise of the cylinder due to heat produced =   °C

Heat produced when the cylinder was rotated   =   kcal

Work done when   newtons act through   metres =   joules

∴ 1 kilocalorie is equivalent to   joules

Suggest sources of error in this experiment and possible ways of reducing their effect on the result.

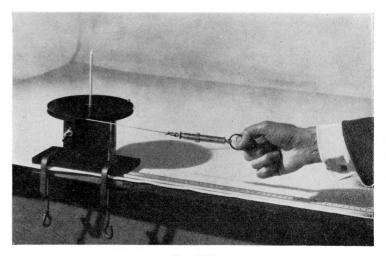

Fig. 220

Experiment 10.4. This experiment is in principle similar to Experiment 10.3, but by turning the handle at a certain speed you can keep a constant force acting round the drum. In this way much more mechanical work can be done on the drum. The temperature rise will be greater and the error smaller.

Measure the heat capacity of the drum using the same method as in the previous experiment. Then fit the drum to the apparatus$_9$ as shown in Fig. 221.

Measure the temperature of the copper drum, and then turn the handle at such a speed that the force on one end of the nylon cord is zero. If the force exerted on the other end of the cord is 100 newtons what force is exerted on the drum? If the circumference of the drum is 0·1 metres, how much work, in joules, is done per revolution?

After 100 revolutions of the handle measure the maximum temperature reached. Find the heat produced by friction and calculate the number of joules required to produce 1 kilocalorie.

Heat needed to raise the temp. of the drum by 1°C =   kcal

Temperature rise of cylinder   =   °C

Heat absorbed by drum   =   kcal

Work done by 100 newtons acting through 100 × 0·1 metres

= 1000 joules

∴   1 kcal is equivalent to   joules

Describe ways of reducing errors in this experiment. How much heat would be produced by (*a*) 50 revolutions of the handle and (*b*) 200 revolutions of the handle? Check your answer.

(Spring balances measuring 100 N are now available$_{18}$.)

As a result of many experiments over many years it has been found that

1 kilocalorie is equivalent to approximately 4200 joules.

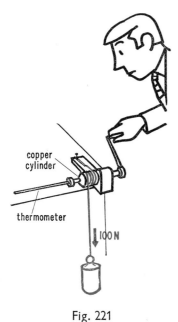

copper
cylinder

thermometer

100 N

Fig. 221

A Joule's a Joule for a' That

Energy is needed to make electric charges flow through a conductor. This energy is transformed into heat when electrons are forced through a piece of wire. When 1 coulomb (6×10^{18} electron charges) flows across a potential difference of 1 volt the energy transformed is 1 joule, so that

Q coulombs flowing across a P.D. of V volts transforms QV joules

$$\therefore \quad \text{Energy} = QV \text{ joules}$$

$$\therefore \quad \text{Energy} = ItV \text{ joules}$$

Experiment 10.5. (*a*) The drum$_9$ used in the last experiment has a built-in electric heater (Fig. 222). You should now pass an electric current through the heater and note the product

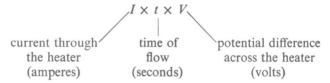

$$I \times t \times V$$

current through the heater (amperes)   time of flow (seconds)   potential difference across the heater (volts)

Adjust those quantities until this product (ItV) is exactly 1000 units and note the temperature rise of the drum. Make certain that the starting temperature is the same as it was in the last experiment.

How does this result compare with that obtained in the last experiment?

(*b*) Repeat the above experiment using a 12 volt a.c. supply and a joulemeter$_9$ (Fig. 223) to measure out 1000 joules.

There is nothing very subtle about this experiment. It is simply to introduce you to the joulemeter, which you probably recognise as the wee brother of the gadget behind the front door at home. The dials on the joulemeter read *joules* whereas the dials on the meter at home read *kilowatt hours*.

$$1 \text{ kilowatt hour} = 10^3 \text{ W} \times 60 \times 60 \text{ s}$$

$$= 10^3 \text{ J/s} \times 3600 \text{ s}$$

$$= 3 \cdot 6 \times 10^6 \frac{\text{J}}{\text{s}} . \text{ s}$$

$$= 3 \cdot 6 \times 10^6 \text{ J}$$

(For experiments with mains-operated equipment a kilowatt hour meter can be calibrated in 'joules per revolution' of the large central disc. A suitable model measures 400 joules per revolution.)

Specific Heat

The heat needed to raise the temperature of a kilogram of a substance by 1°C is called the *specific heat* (*s*). You already know the specific heat of water as 1 kcal. As we now know that 1 kilocalorie is equal to 4200 joules, we shall from now on take the specific heat of water as 4200 joules per kilogram per degree Celsius.

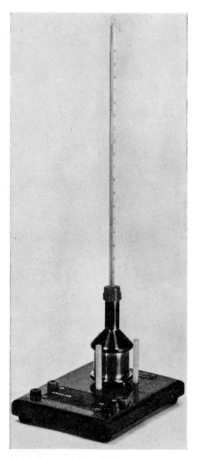

Fig. 222

Fig. 223

From the previous work you should be able to complete this table. (5)

Heat needed to raise temp. of 1 kg of a substance by 1°C is   ***s** J*

Heat needed to raise temp. of m kg of a substance by 1°C is   *J*

Heat needed to raise temp. of m kg of a substance by ΔT°C is   *J*

We will now use joules to measure all forms of energy.

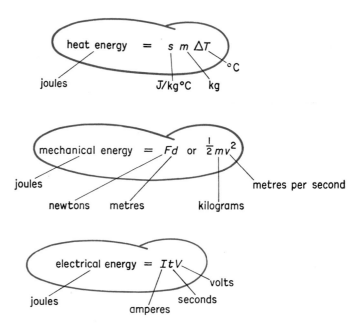

heat energy $= s\,m\,\Delta T$

joules   J/kg°C   kg   °C

mechanical energy $= Fd$ or $\frac{1}{2}mv^2$

joules   newtons   metres   kilograms   metres per second

electrical energy $= ItV$

joules   amperes   seconds   volts

Power

Here are a few examples showing the approximate rate at which chemical energy is changed from food in your body into other forms (1 watt = 1 joule per second).

Asleep	75 watts
Sitting	150 watts
Walking	300 watts
Running	600 watts

In the case of an accelerating car, chemical energy in petrol is changed to mechanical energy at the following rates approximately.

Mini	25 kilowatts
Jaguar	150 kilowatts

The First Law of Thermodynamics

The idea that the total amount of energy remains the same although it is forever changing from one form to another is called the *conservation of energy*. It is sometimes called the First Law of Thermodynamics and can be stated thus: mechanical energy can be changed to heat or heat to mechanical energy at a fixed rate of exchange.

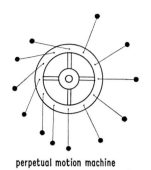

perpetual motion machine

Fig. 224

Fig. 225

Perpetual motion machines of many kinds have been suggested. The intention was that they would keep moving without feeding in energy. A satellite will of course do that! To be of any use, however, a perpetual motion machine would have to provide energy, free of charge, to do useful work. *Can you see why, if the first law of thermodynamics is correct, it would be impossible to build a perpetual motion machine?* (6)

Fig. 224 shows a proposed device. The spokes are pivoted between stops on the rim and each spoke has a mass attached to the end. *Can you suggest why it was thought that this wheel would rotate continually?* (7) *What are the snags?* (8)

Making Heat Work

Practically all the important work dealing with the production of heat energy from mechanical energy has been done during the last 200 years. The reverse operation, that of obtaining mechanical energy from heat energy, has, on the other hand, been studied for at least 2000 years. In this field progress was made largely by trial and error.

In the first century A.D. Hero of Alexandria constructed a system of pulleys and ropes, which magically opened the doors of a temple when a fire was lit on the altar. The doors closed when the fire went out.

The principle of Hero's system is illustrated in Fig. 226. The bunsen burner represents the fire on the altar and the pointer the door. The rest of the gubbins was concealed below the temple floor. *Can you work out its operation?* (9)

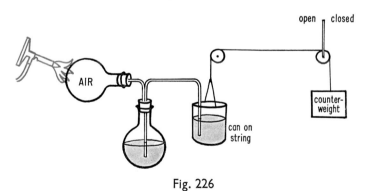

Fig. 226

Hero also made a steam turbine, a model of which you saw earlier in the course (Book 1, Fig. 209). During the Dark Ages Hero's gadgets were buried, and it was not until some 15 centuries later that they were dug up and attempts made to copy and improve them.

Leonardo da Vinci (1452–1519) used the convection currents above a flame to turn a vaned wheel, and during the 17th century various attempts were made to use heat to drive machines. One of these was a crude kind of impulse turbine rather like the one illustrated in Book 1, Fig. 206.

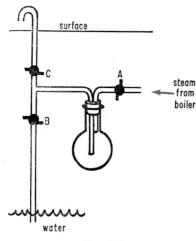

surface

C

A

steam
from
boiler

B

water

Fig. 227

The Steam Revolution

It would be difficult to say who first thought of using steam to operate machinery, but most of the inventors seem at least to have had the same source of inspiration. They watched a soup pot or kettle lid in action! As early as 1601 Giovanni della Porta spoke of the 'force of steam when confined' and the reduced pressure created when steam condensed.

In 1652 the Second Marquis of Worcester was accused of spying and sent to the Tower of London. While there he is thought to have devised an engine for pumping water out of coal mines. His design was published in a book, but there is no evidence that he ever really built such a machine. The increasing number of coal mines in use made the need for such a pump very urgent and, when in 1698 Thomas Savery built the first steam engine or pump, he was accused by some of having copied the machine designed by the Marquis of Worcester. The principle of Savery's pump is shown in Fig. 227.

Assume that the steam boiler is fitted with a safety valve so that closing valve A cuts off the steam to the pump. If valves A and B are open and C closed, steam will be forced into the flask. *If now valves A and C are closed and B left open, what will happen when the steam condenses?* (10) *Can you think of a third stage during which water will be forced to the surface?* (11)

The Newcomen Engine

The high-pressure steam cylinder used in the Savery pump had proved to be extremely dangerous. At the beginning of the 18th century an English blacksmith, Thomas Newcomen (1663–1729), invented an atmospheric engine which operated at low pressure, thus reducing the casualties caused by bursting boilers.

The Newcomen engine had no revolving parts. It simply groaned up and down as it pumped water from the mine. This enormous, heavy, noisy brute was extremely greedy on coal but it had no rival for half a century. Fortunately such engines were always built where coal was plentiful!

Fig. 228 shows a simplified picture of the engine. With valves A and C closed steam is allowed into the cylinder via valve B. The piston moves up, and when it is at the top of its stroke valve B is closed and valve C opened to allow water to spray into the cylinder. This causes the steam to condense so that the pressure in the cylinder is reduced. The atmospheric pressure then pushes the piston down.

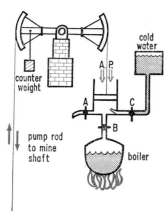

cold
water

counter
weight

A. P.

A

C

B

pump rod
to mine
shaft

boiler

Fig. 228

Valves B and C are then closed and valve A opened to allow the water to run out of the cylinder. The whole cycle is then repeated. As the valves had to be operated by a boy only a few strokes per minute were possible with this engine. Humphrey Potter was one such boy who found the job interfered with his games, and so he rigged up an automatic valve gear which enabled him to play marbles with his friends while the engine operated on its own! As there were no trades unions in those days Humphrey lost his job.

James Watt (*1736–1819*)

Watt began his career as an instrument maker at Glasgow University. At one time he was asked to repair a Newcomen

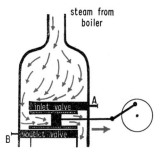

steam from boiler

Fig. 229

engine and was surprised at the tremendous amount of steam required to operate it. He found that about 85 per cent of this steam was being used to raise the temperature of the cylinder which had just been cooled by the cold water, and decided to modify the system so that the cylinder was kept at steam temperature all the time. To do this the steam had to be condensed *outside* the cylinder. Watt first took out a patent for his improved engine in 1769 but this was just the beginning of a series. His later models were about eight times as efficient as the Newcomen engine.

The reciprocating engine shown in Fig. 229 is similar in principle to Watt's later engines. The steam, at high pressure, pushes the piston and is then allowed to escape during the next half cycle. At the appropriate times rods A and B are pushed to reverse the movement of the piston. *Can you work out* when *these valves should be operated?* (12) Successors to Humphrey Potter have of course applied automation to these operations. Watt discovered that by closing the inlet valve early and allowing the steam to expand in the cylinder a much greater efficiency was obtained: even so it was still of the order of 10 per cent or less.

Watt's engines started the Industrial Revolution and soon cloth was being spun and woven using steam. The young Scots engineer, William Murdoch, was employed by Watt's firm in Cornwall. He decided to build a small steam engine and put in on wheels. In order to test it out in secret, Murdoch chose the long straight path leading to the church outside the town. He had not, however, reckoned on the vicar being in the vicinity at the time! When confronted in the dark by this noisy monster belching fire and smoke, the vicar imagined it was 'the Evil One himself' (Fig. 230).

Another engineer, Captain Richard Trevithick, built a steam road locomotive which had its trial run on Christmas Eve, 1801, and its last run four days later! (Fig. 231). While he was celebrating the success of the new 'walking, puffing devil' at a local inn the fire was left burning. The water soon boiled away and 'nothing that was combustible remained either of the engine or the

Fig. 230

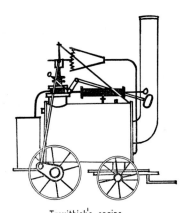

Trevithick's engine

Fig. 231

Fig. 232
Crown Copyright. Science Museum, London

house'! Later, Trevithick made another engine and exhibited it in London.

George Stephenson, an English engineer, then built a steam engine to run on rails (Fig. 232). In 1814 it hauled 10 coal trucks at a speed of 5 miles per hour. The steam locomotive was born.

The Hot Air Engine

In addition to their use in mines and in locomotives steam engines were becoming more and more popular in ships. Unfortunately, about half of them ended in disaster when their boilers burst! Inventors therefore started to consider air rather than steam as a working substance.

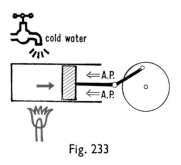

Fig. 233

The principle of the hot-air engine is very simple. If a cylinder containing air (Fig. 233) is heated, the air expands and pushes the piston to the right. If then the cylinder is cooled the air will contract and the atmospheric pressure will push the cylinder to the left. A method of realising this in practice was invented by a Scots minister, Robert Stirling, in 1827. Instead of heating and cooling the same part of the cylinder, he continually heated one part and cooled another. He then arranged a *displacer* to push the air from the hot to the cold part as required. His method is shown diagrammatically in Fig. 234.

The displacer is a light cylindrical tube sealed at both ends. It slides freely in the cylinder and allows air past. When the displacer is in position A, the air is heated and the piston is pushed to the right. If now the displacer is pushed to position B, the air in the cylinder is displaced to the right-hand side where it is cooled, and the piston moves to the left. As with the valve in Watt's engine, the displacer is in practice moved automatically by connecting it to the flywheel of the engine.

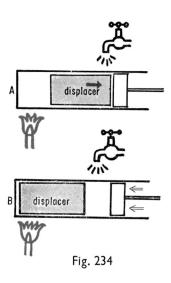

Fig. 234

In some versions of the Stirling hot-air engine, such as the model shown in Fig. 235, the piston and displacer are in separate connected cylinders. In the model shown here a methylated spirit lamp heats one end of the cylinder and the other end is cooled by convection.

Hot-air engines were reasonably efficient but they were large and extremely heavy. In 1854 John Ericsson, the inventor of the ship's propeller, fitted a huge 8 cylinder engine in a small boat. It sighed and sank! One hot-air engine capable of developing only 2 horsepower weighed 4 tons. Recently the Stirling engine has been brought up to date by Philips of Eindhoven. A 4 cylinder experimental version now produces 360 horse power.

Fig. 235

Modern Engines

During the latter half of the 19th century and the first half of the 20th century many new forms of heat engines appeared. Perhaps the most revolutionary was the internal combustion engine (see model in Book 1, Fig. 133). Instead of the fuel being **burned** outside the engine, as in the steam and hot air engines, the fuel is burned inside the cylinder itself. The most common form is the four-stroke petrol engine devised in 1886 by Nikolaus Otto.

Suck, Squeeze, Bang, Blow

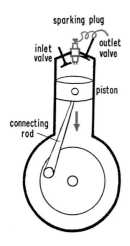

Fig. 236

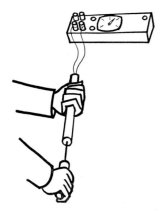

Fig. 237

In this engine an explosive mixture of petrol vapour and air is produced by a carburetter (see Book Two, page 12). As the piston moves down (Fig. 236) it creates a partial vacuum. The mixture is then forced, by atmospheric pressure, to enter the engine cylinder through the inlet valve. The outlet valve is closed.

With both valves closed the piston moves up to compress the mixture. An electric spark then ignites the vapour mixture which burns rapidly (explodes) at a very high temperature. The heat produced causes the gas pressure to build up rapidly and this pushes the piston down as the gas expands.

Can you suggest the fourth stroke of the cycle? (13) *Which valves, if any, will be open during* (a) *the third and* (b) *the fourth stroke?* (14) *Which is the power stroke?* (15) *What keeps the piston moving up and down during the other three strokes?* (16) *Would you expect an internal combustion engine to be more or less efficient than a steam engine?* (17) *Why?* (18)

Demonstration 10.6. Insert a copper/constantan thermocouple in the end of a bicycle pump and plug the hole with plasticine. A sensitive galvanometer$_{14}$ must be used to indicate any change of temperature. What happens when the air inside the pump is compressed? (Fig. 237).

Can you explain the result in terms of molecular collisions? (Book 1, page 90).

In 1897, the German engineer, Rudolph Diesel, invented another internal combustion engine. It uses a four-stroke cycle, similar to the Otto cycle, but operates on fuel oil instead of petrol. There is no sparking plug in the Diesel engine, ignition being produced automatically when the fuel oil, which is injected at a very high pressure, is compressed further by the piston. Modern internal combustion engines can have efficiencies as high as 30–35 per cent.

Turbines

Practically all the large stationary steam engines in use today are turbines. By passing steam through a series of vanes of increasing size, much more mechanical work can be obtained from a given amount of heat energy than is possible with the reciprocating steam engine. Modern turbines (Fig. 238) owe their origin to the British engineer, Sir Charles A. Parsons (1845–1931).

Modern steam turbines with efficiencies of about 30 per cent compare very favourably with reciprocating steam engines in which the efficiency is less than 20 per cent.

Project 10.7. Devise an experiment to find the rate at which heat is supplied by a methylated spirit or gas burner used to operate a model steam engine$_{15}$ (e.g. Mamod SE3). Express this in joules per second (watts).

Now use the steam engine to raise a small load, and find the rate at which work is done in raising the load. Express this also in newton-metres per second (watts). From these results find the efficiency of the engine.

Fig. 238

By courtesy of C. A. Parsons & Co. Ltd.

If a permanent-magnet electric motor[15] (e.g. Kako No. 5) is used as a dynamo, this will operate a torch bulb (Fig. 239). Using an ammeter and voltmeter find the power of the bulb and hence the overall efficiency of the 'generating station'.

Fig. 239

Project 10.8. Use an electric motor to raise a load, and measure the input (electrical energy) and the output (mechanical energy). Find the efficiency of the electric motor.

(Kits are available commercially[3.20].)

Transfer of Heat

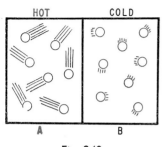

HOT   COLD

A   B

Fig. 240

When a hot and a cold substance are brought into contact the chances of the heat in the cold substance being transferred to the hot so that the hot becomes hotter and the cold colder are so remote that we can assume that it never happens. The vigorous (hot) molecules transfer some of their energy by collision to the cold molecules, and this process continues until the rate of flow of heat from A to B (Fig. 240) is the same as the rate of flow of heat from B to A. The two substances are then said to be in thermal equilibrium. The average kinetic energy ($\frac{1}{2} m\overline{v^2}$) of the molecules in A is the same as the average kinetic energy of the molecules in B. That is, the two substances are at the same temperature. The second law of thermodynamics can be stated in many ways, but one of the simplest forms is that 'heat will not flow of its own accord from a colder to a hotter substance'.

There is enough heat energy in the sea to supply all our energy needs but we cannot easily make use of it. The most useless form of heat is heat at low temperatures. In fact, this is the ultimate fate of practically all the energy used on the Earth.

Summary

The laws of thermodynamics can be summarised as follows:
Law 1. Heat and mechanical energy are interchangeable at a fixed rate of exchange (1 kilocalorie = 4200 joules).
Law 2. Heat does not of its own accord flow from a cold to a hot substance.
Law 3. It is impossible to reach absolute zero.

Problems

19. *Why is it necessary for a space capsule to be fitted with a heat shield?*

20. *Suggest experiments which show that sound and light are forms of energy.*

21. *In what way is heat responsible for (a) the erosion of the land (b) winds (c) volcanoes? Where does the heat come from in each case?*

22. *A boy defined energy as 'anything which can be changed to heat'! Would you accept this?*

23. *If an electric fan is switched on in a heat-insulated room will it cool the room?*

24. *If your brother asks you to close the door as it is 'letting in the cold', what would you say? ('Shut it yourself', is not the answer required!)*

25. *Why must a starter be used to start a petrol engine?*

26. *Steam locomotives are still only about 7 per cent efficient yet electric locomotives can be about 95 per cent efficient. Why then are not all trains powered by electricity?*

27. *An efficient generating station may be 25 per cent efficient. If the energy changes are chemical → heat → mechanical → electrical, which is the least efficient stage?*

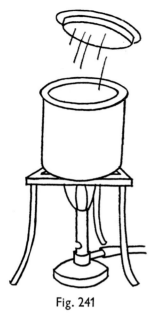

Fig. 241

Fig. 242

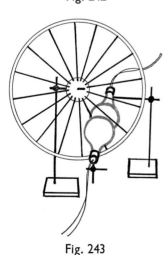

Fig. 243

Optional Extras

Science Steps In

Apart from the efforts of James Watt no serious attempt had been made at the beginning of the 19th century to study the principles governing the efficiency of engines. A young French artillery officer, Sadi Carnot, was the first person to investigate this scientifically. When he was 28 he wrote his only book. It was a short volume of 100 pages, and yet it has been called the most marvellous 100 pages in the history of science. He did not investigate any particular type of engine, for example steam or hot air, but concerned himself rather with the more fundamental problem of how much *work* could be obtained from a certain quantity of *heat*.

Any device which changes heat energy to mechanical energy he called a *heat engine*. Here are a few examples.

Experiment 10.9. (*a*) A coffee tin can be used as a heat engine (Fig. 241). The air is heated and the work is done as the lid takes off.
(*b*) A lump of metal suspended by an elastic band can be raised vertically by heating the elastic (Fig. 242). This is a heat engine.

Project 10.10. You may like to construct a wheel with elastic spokes (use, for example, the rim of a bicycle wheel). If the wheel is fixed to rotate in a vertical plane and infra red heaters are placed close to the spokes on one side of the hub (Fig. 243), the bands will contract and the wheel will rotate. Can you explain why it rotates? Is this a heat engine?

Carnot compared the heat engine, in which mechanical work is done by heat, to a water wheel, in which work is done by water falling from a high level. He said that in the case of the water wheel the work done depends on the difference in the water levels above and below the wheel, and in the case of the heat engine the work done depends on the temperature difference between the heat going into the engine and the heat coming out.

If you start with mechanical energy it is possible to change it *all* into heat, but if you start with heat energy only *part* of it can be changed into mechanical energy. In other words no heat engine can use all the heat put into it. Cars have water-cooled radiators to carry off the unused heat, and locomotives release warm steam into the atmosphere. Carnot showed that even under ideal conditions (no frictional losses etc.) the maximum efficiency of any heat engine could never be 100 per cent, and the efficiency could only be high if the *difference* between the temperatures at which heat enters and leaves the engine were as great as possible.

Working on the caloric theory Carnot believed that the amount of heat going into an engine was equal to the amount of heat coming out of the engine. A few years later Lord Kelvin and Rudolf Clausius interpreted Carnot's work in terms of the mechanical theory. Carnot's conclusion, however, remained true. It is the difference between the temperatures at which heat enters and leaves the engine and not the working substance (for example, gas, steam, etc.) that determines the efficiency of the engine.

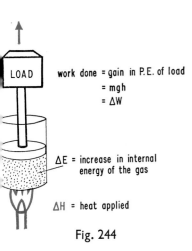

LOAD work done = gain in P.E. of load
= mgh
= ΔW

ΔE = increase in internal
energy of the gas

ΔH = heat applied

Fig. 244

Why, you may ask, is it not possible to change all the heat energy into mechanical energy? This is a very difficult question, and we can only give a clue as to the direction along which the answer may be found.

Some forms of energy are more useful than others as they can very easily be transformed. Electricity can produce mechanical energy, heat, light or sound at the touch of a button. It is not so easy to use gas to operate a vacuum cleaner or a TV. set. A small methylated spirit lamp will drive a model steam engine, which will in turn operate a dynamo to generate electric current. On the other hand a bath full of tepid water, containing much more heat energy than the boiler of the steam engine, cannot be used to drive machinery. Heat at high temperature is useful heat, whereas heat at low temperature is of little value. Consider the following simple heat engine (Fig. 244).

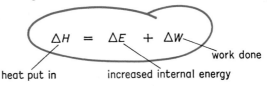

heat put in   increased internal energy

$$\Delta H = \Delta E + \Delta W$$

work done

If a certain amount of heat at a high temperature (ΔH) is put into a heat engine so that a load is raised, then some work (ΔW) is done. The gas in the cylinder is, however, heated up and gains what we might call *internal energy*, (ΔE), that is, the molecules of the gas speed up. Clearly ΔW is less than ΔH by the amount of heat given to the gas. In order to make our simple engine drive a wheel, as in the case of the Stirling engine, we must now *remove* the heat from the gas, so that the piston can return to the bottom of the cylinder. The heat removed is wasted energy as far as doing useful work is concerned.

Molecular Chaos

The second law of thermodynamics can be considered from the molecular point of view. To do this we really need the help of the mathematicians and, in particular, we need statistics. Although we cannot deal with this subject at present the following illustration may give you a clue which can be followed up later (Fig. 245).

Imagine that you pour 75 black balls into a glass jar and then pour 75 white balls on top of them. The jar is photographed, shaken for a few seconds and photographed again. It is shaken again, photographed again, etc. Fig. 245 shows five photographs taken after a number of such shakings. *Can you say in what order the photographs were taken?* (28) *What made you decide on this order?* (29) *If the jar were shaken another 1000 times what would happen?* (30) *How long would you have to shake it to obtain an arrangement like Fig. 245 (c)?* (31)

Scientists call the original arrangement (c) *order* and the final arrangement (e) *disorder*. Left to themselves, things always become more and more disordered. Imagine that you are watching a movie film of, say, a stone breaking a window. If things are becoming more and more disordered you know that the film is running forwards. If they are becoming more and more ordered it is in reverse.

(a)   (b)   (c)

(d)   (e)

Fig. 245

Fig. 246

Imagine a lead ball falling freely (Fig. 246). As it drops all the molecules are, on the average, moving in *one direction*. This is ordered motion and the kinetic energy of such a moving body can be usefully employed. The electrons in a wire carrying electric current move along, on the average, in one direction, and again useful work can be done. Mechanical kinetic energy and electrical energy are *high quality* energies, which can both be easily changed into other forms.

When the ball strikes the ground the *ordered* movement of the molecules changes on impact to *disordered* (random) movement. The molecules now move in all directions in a higgledy-piggledy way. The ordered molecular movement (kinetic energy) has changed to disordered molecular movement (heat). The reverse procedure is so unlikely as to be, to all intents and purposes, impossible. That is, the molecules moving at random are hardly likely to arrange themselves so that they all act in one direction causing the stationary (hot) ball suddenly to jump up in the air and become cold! Left to themselves, then, things tend to become more and more disordered, never the reverse. A heat engine is a device which is able to change some disorder (heat) into order (kinetic energy), but, as we have seen, it can never transform it all.

Visual Aids

Charts: Diesel Engine$_{24}$ C590.
Filmstrips: Heat Energy$_{22}$. S14.
     The Internal Combustion Engine$_{23}$ 09.23.
     Jet Propulsion$_{23}$ 09.68.
16 mm Films: Thermodynamics$_{23}$ 20.3875.
     The Steam Turbine$_{23}$ 70.3582.
     Jet Propulsion$_{23}$ 20.7342.
     The Diesel Story$_{25,26}$.
     An Introduction to the Heat Engine$_{25,26}$.
     How the Motor Car Works. Part 1, The Engine$_{25,26}$.
     Mechanical and Thermal Energy (P.S.S.C.)$_{26}$ D2636/2.

Freedom and the State

CHAPTER 11

Specific Heat

When a substance such as water is heated two changes can take place: a change of *temperature* or a change of *state*. These changes correspond to changes in the kinetic energy and the potential energy of the molecules. As the temperature rises the kinetic energy of the molecules increases. When a certain temperature is reached, for example the boiling point of water, adding heat causes no increase in the temperature. The additional energy is used to separate the molecules from each other so that they have more freedom to move around on their own. The substance has changed its *state*.

The Scots physician and chemist, Joseph Black (1728–1799), was the first man clearly to distinguish these two effects of heat. The heat needed to change the temperature of 1 kilogram of a substance by 1 degree Celsius is called the *specific heat* of the substance, and the heat needed to change the *state* of 1 kilogram of a solid to a liquid, or a liquid to a vapour, is called the *latent heat*.

In the following experiment you can find the specific heat of several liquids and solids. Remember that

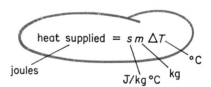

$$\text{heat supplied} = s\, m\, \Delta T$$

joules   J/kg °C   kg   °C

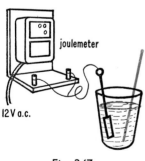

joulemeter

12 V a.c.

Fig. 247

Experiment 11.1. (*a*) Pour some methylated spirit into an Aero-cup$_4$, and insert a 12 v immersion heater$_3$ as shown (Fig. 247). Make sure the heater is totally immersed before switching it on. Measure the temperature of the liquid and then use a joulemeter to supply (say) 1000 joules of heat to the liquid. Read the maximum temperature obtained.

Use these results to calculate the specific heat of methylated spirit. What assumptions have you made?

Repeat this experiment for other liquids such as brine, olive oil or paraffin oil.

(*b*) As an alternative to the joulemeter an ammeter, voltmeter and stopwatch can be used. The product ItV gives the heat in joules.

(*c*) A third method avoids the use of all meters. Using the known value of the specific heat of water (4200 J/kg°C) calibrate the immersion heater with a stop watch. Once you know how many joules per second it supplies, the above experiments can be conducted with the heater and a stopwatch. You must, of course, make certain that the supply voltage remains constant throughout.

Experiment 11.2. (*a*) Take a 1 kilogram cylinder of aluminium, and fix it on an immersion heater as shown in Fig. 248. Pour a drop

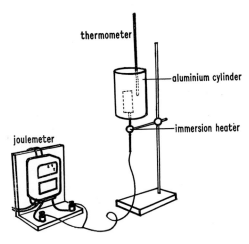

Fig. 248

of oil in the small hole and insert a thermometer. Read the temperature before and after passing (say) 1000 joules into the aluminium. From these results calculate the specific heat of aluminium.

Repeat the experiment with cylinders$_3$ of other metals.

(*b*) Alternatively use an ammeter, voltmeter and stopwatch or a calibrated heater.

Approximate Values for Some Specific Heats

Air (s.t.p.) at constant pressure	1000 J/kg °C
Water	4200 ,, ,,
Methylated spirit	2300 ,, ,,
Paraffin	2200 ,, ,,
Turpentine	1800 ,, ,,
Mercury	140 ,, ,,
Paraffin wax	2900 ,, ,,
Ice	2000 ,, ,,
Aluminium	880 ,, ,,
Glass (crown)	670 ,, ,,
Iron	440 ,, ,,
Copper	380 ,, ,,
Brass	370 ,, ,,
Lead	130 ,, ,,

Project 11.3. Use a test tube and some water to estimate the number of joules obtained by burning a match. Is your result an over- or under-estimate?

Problems

1. *If 200 grams of water at 40°C are mixed with 100 grams of water at 10°C and no heat is lost, what is the final temperature?*

2. *If an immersion heater heats 300 grams of water for 2 minutes and the temperature rises by 30°C find the power rating of the heater in watts.*

3. *The food a 50 kilogram woman eats in a day provides her with 3000 kilocalories. If the same amount of heat were taken in by 50 kilograms of water at normal blood temperature (37°C), what would be the final temperature? Why does the woman not reach this temperature?*

4. *If a lead ball is dropped on a hard surface the ball is deformed, and we can assume all the kinetic energy is changed to heat in the ball. From what height must the ball be dropped to raise its temperature by 2°C?*

5. *A car of mass 850 kilograms is brought to rest from 20 metres per second by applying the brakes. If all the kinetic energy is changed to heat in the brake drums, find the temperature rise if each of the four iron drums has a mass of 5 kilograms.*

6. *To find the temperature of a furnace you might heat a lump of metal until it reached the temperature of the furnace and then transfer it to water. Suppose a lump of metal with a heat capacity of 100 J/°C was transferred to 1 kilogram of water and the temperature of the water rose from 20°C to 50°C: find (a) the heat gained by the water, (b) the heat lost by the metal and (c) the temperature of the furnace.*

7. *In a paddle wheel experiment two masses, each of 10 kilograms, fall through 5 metres. If they fall 10 times and the water and container are equivalent to 4 kilograms of water as far as absorbing heat is concerned, find the temperature change produced assuming Joules result: 1 kilocalorie = 4200 joules.*

8. *A swimmer uses 10^5 joules of chemical energy in 30 seconds. If only 25 per cent of this energy is used in moving him through the water and in that time he swims 40 metres, find the average resistance to his motion. What happens to the other 75 per cent of this energy?*

9. *A meteor of mass 20 kilograms slows down from 450 metres per second to 50 metres per second by passing through the Earth's atmosphere. How much heat is generated?*

10. *An 80 kg climber can climb (vertically) at a rate of 0·2 metres per second. What is his gain of potential energy after a 3 hour climb? If 25 per cent of the chemical energy he uses is transformed to potential energy, how many kilocalories of food should he eat before the climb? (1 kilocalorie = 4200 joules).*

11. *1 kilowatt hour (or unit) of electrical energy costs 2d. 1 Therm (that is 10^5 BThU or $1·055 \times 10^8$ joules) of gas energy costs 2s. Compare the cost of heating by gas and electricity.*

How would off-peak electricity at 0·8d. per unit compare with gas on a reduced rate of 1s. 6d. per Therm?

12. *If all the electricity produced by a hydro-electric power station were used to heat the water passing through the turbines could the water temperature be raised to its boiling point? Show rough figures to explain the answer you give.*

The Price of Freedom

To change a liquid to a gas (vapour) energy is needed. Can you say where the energy comes from in each of the following cases?

Experiment 11.4. (*a*) Pour a drop of volatile liquid such as ether or petrol on the back of your hand and wave it around.

(*b*) Measure the temperature of ether in a closed bottle and in an open dish. Can you explain the results in terms of energetic molecules leaving the surface?

(*c*) Soak a piece of blotting paper in ether and wrap it round the bulb of a thermometer. Note the reading produced.

Experiment 11.5. Place a thermocouple in some methylated spirits. Explain the meter reading when the thermocouple is taken out of the methylated spirits.

Experiment 11.6. Place a watch glass on a few drops of water on the bench. Now pour some ether into the watch glass and blow air across it or through it. What happens and why?

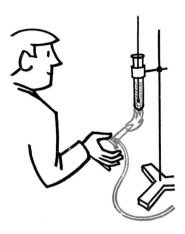

Fig. 249

When a liquid evaporates it is because some of the faster-moving molecules leave the surface and shoot into the air above. The average speed of the molecules left behind in the liquid is therefore less: that is, the average kinetic energy ($\frac{1}{2}m\,\overline{v^2}$) is less and so the temperature is lower.

Experiment 11.7. (*a*) Gently heat some naphthalene powder in a test tube (Fig. 249) until the temperature reaches 100°C. Now remove the bunsen burner and read the temperature of the naphthalene at $\frac{1}{2}$ minute intervals. When not actually reading the temperature stir the naphthalene gently with the thermometer.

Plot a graph of your results and comment on its shape.

(*b*) This experiment can be conducted very much more quickly with a calibrated thermocouple (Fig. 250) and a small test tube of naphthalene.

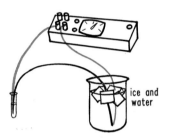

ice and water

Fig. 250

Latent Heat of Fusion

In the solid state the molecules vibrate to and fro in the crystal lattice (Fig. 251). To overcome the attraction between the molecules energy is needed. This gives the molecules more freedom to move around in the liquid state (Fig. 252).

Project 11.8. Place a thimble full of water and a thimble full of liquid paraffin wax in the freezing compartment of a refrigerator and explain the results obtained.

Would ice float on water? (13) *Would solid paraffin wax float on liquid paraffin wax?* (14). *Why don't lakes freeze to the bottom?* (15) (Book 1, page 83).

In the following experiment you can find how much heat is needed to melt 1 kilogram of ice, that is, to change it from a solid at 0°C into a liquid at 0°C. This quantity is called the latent heat of fusion of ice.

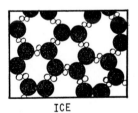

ICE

Fig. 251

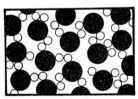

water molecules

Fig. 252

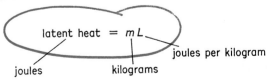

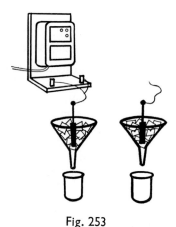

Fig. 253

Experiment 11.9. Place a 50 W immersion heater₃ in a filter funnel and surround the heater with small pieces of ice as shown in Fig. 253. Supply (say) 4000 joules to the ice and weigh the water produced. Can you suggest why a second piece of similar apparatus is shown and how it would be used in this experiment?

From your results find the latent heat of fusion of ice.

Practical Puzzle

16. *A body floating in water displaces its own weight of water. If a lump of ice is floating on a tumbler filled to the brim with water, will the water overflow when the ice melts? Explain.*

Problems

17. *Two similar houses stand side by side. One roof is covered with snow and the other is clear. Give reasons for saying (a) the snow-covered house would be warmer inside or (b) the other would be warmer inside. State any assumptions you make.*

18. *Ice is formed on the side of a black and white painted traffic signal. When the sun shines will the ice on the black or the white parts melt first? Explain your answer.*

19. *Would you cool a can of water more quickly by placing it on ice or placing ice in it? Explain the answer you give.*

20. *A number of rectangular blocks, all having the same mass (500 g) and the same cross-sectional area are made from aluminium, zinc, copper, iron and lead. If these blocks are heated to 100°C and then placed on a large flat horizontal surface of ice, what will happen?*

21. *'When water freezes it gives out heat'. Is this statement correct and, if so, where does the heat come from?*

22. *Why do rivers and lochs not freeze solid as soon as the atmospheric temperature reaches 0°C?*

23. *Why is solid carbon dioxide called dry ice?*

In the following problems take the latent heat of fusion of ice as 3.34×10^5 J/kg.

24. *How much heat is needed to melt 50 g of ice at 0°C?*

25. *If water at 60°C is mixed with an equal mass of ice at 0°C, find the final temperature.*

26. *What is the least mass of water at 50°C which you would have to add to 10 grams of ice at 0°C to melt it?*

27. *If a 100 gram bullet travelling at 500 metres per second enters a block of ice, estimate the mass which would melt.*

28. *If 0·4 kilograms of lead shot at 100°C is poured into a hole in a large block of ice at 0°C, how much ice will melt? What will be the final temperature of the lead shot?*

Latent Heat of Vaporisation

If the liquid molecules are to be set free to move around on their own (gaseous state), they require a great deal of energy to overcome the forces holding them together (Fig. 254).

The heat needed to change 1 kg of boiling water into steam at the same temperature is called the *latent heat of vaporisation* of water. You can find it from the following experiment.

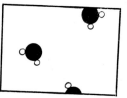

water molecules in air (STEAM)

Fig. 254

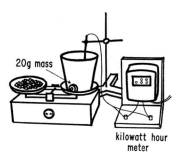

20g mass

kilowatt hour
meter

Fig. 255

Demonstration 11.10. Place an expanded polystyrene flower pot on one side of a balance. Partially fill the pot with water and suspend a 300 watt immersion heater$_3$ in the water as shown. Use a kilowatt-hour meter to measure the energy supplied to the immersion heater by first noting how many joules are supplied per revolution of the large central wheel (Fig. 255).

Switch on the current and, when the water is boiling, pour lead shot on the other pan until balance is obtained. At this instant note the meter reading.

Now place a 20 gram mass beside the flower pot. The water will continue boiling until, when 20 grams of water have boiled off, the sides will balance again. When this happens note the new meter reading and thus find the number of joules used. From these results calculate the latent heat of vaporisation of water. Why is this much greater than the latent heat of fusion of ice?

(*b*) If a suitable kilowatt-hour meter is not available the immersion heater can be calibrated by finding the temperature rise of a known mass of water in a given time.

Problems

29. *If in a central heating system steam enters a radiator at 100°C and water leaves the radiator at 100°C, can this radiator heat a room? Explain your answer.*

30. *Why do athletes when wet with perspiration protect themselves from draughts?*

31. *A tin of water floats in a pan of boiling water. Can the water in the tin boil? Explain your answer.*

32. *'It's not the heat, it's the humidity'. Comment on this statement.*

33. *Hot curry makes you sweat. Would you therefore prefer to eat it in a hot dry or a hot humid climate? Why?*

34. *Why does a dog's tongue hang out on a hot day?*

35. *Why are fogs often worst in the morning, and why do they tend to disappear in the afternoon?*

36 *Potatoes are boiling in a saucepan. Will 'turning up the gas' cook the potatoes more quickly?*

37. *Why does a porous pot keep liquids cool?*

In the following questions take the latent heat of vaporisation of water as $2 \cdot 26 \times 10^6$ J/kg.

38. *A 300 watt immersion heater is used to heat water to its boiling point. The heater is left on for 5 minutes after the water boils. What mass of water will be boiled off in these 5 minutes?*

39. *A 2 kilogram iron bar is taken from a forge at 900°C and plunged into a pail containing 10 kilograms of water at 70°C. How much steam can be produced?*

40. *A steam heating system delivers steam at atmospheric pressure and 100°C to radiators. When the water eventually returns to the boiler its temperature is 85°C. What mass of steam is needed to produce 10^8 joules?*

41. *A large polystyrene flower pot contains 1 kilogram of water at 20°C. Steam at 100°C is blown into the water and the temperature reaches 40°C. Find the mass of steam used.*

Changes in the Melting Point

From the following experiments can you find how impurities and pressure affect the melting point of ice?

Experiment 11.11. Add salt to a mixture of ice and water and investigate the new melting point.

Experiment 11.12. Can you think of a simple way of applying a very large pressure to a block of ice? Do this and say what you think has happened to the melting point of ice under pressure.

Changes in the Boiling Point

Investigate the change in the boiling point of water when impurities are added or the pressure is varied.

Experiment 11.13. Find how the addition of salt to water affects its boiling point.

Experiment 11.14. Boil some water in a round-bottomed flask and insert a stopper and thermometer in the flask. Invert the flask and pour cold water over it (Fig. 256). What will happen to the pressure inside? Why? Does the water continue to boil at a higher or a lower temperature under reduced pressure?

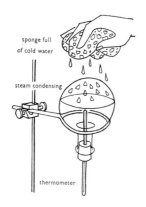

sponge full
of cold water

steam condensing

thermometer

Fig. 256

The boiling point of a liquid in air is defined as the temperature at which the pressure of the vapour is equal to the external atmospheric pressure above the liquid. If the pressure above the liquid is reduced, as in the above experiment, molecules escaping from the liquid surface can produce a vapour pressure equal to this reduced pressure at a much lower temperature; that is, the boiling point is reduced.

Problems

42. *Explain the use of anti-freeze in car radiators, and of salt on icy pavements.*

43. *Why cannot tea be brewed in the usual way on a very high mountain?*

44. *Is it easier to skate on ice when the air temperature is just below freezing point or when it is very much lower than this? Why?*

45. *Water expands when it freezes and the freezing point decreases with pressure. Can you suggest a molecular explanation for these two phenomena?*

46. *If water were boiled in a pressure cooker, would the boiling point be greater or less than 100°C?*

Optional Extras

Refrigerators

When the gas in a refrigerator is compressed it changes to a liquid, and in so doing *gives out* its latent heat. If the liquid is then allowed to expand into a much larger space, it changes back to a gas and so it *takes in* its latent heat. By continually pumping a substance like Freon round a circuit heat can be taken in at one place and given out at another (Fig. 257).

Why is the freezing compartment at the top *of a refrigerator?* (47) *Would you agree with the housewife who leaves her fridge door open in the summer to 'cool the kitchen'?* (48) *Explain your answer.* (49)

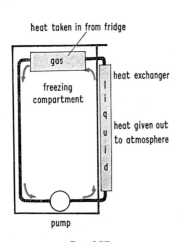

heat taken in from fridge

gas

heat exchanger

freezing
compartment

l
i
q
u
i
d

heat given out
to atmosphere

pump

Fig. 257

Heat Pumps

If we want to make water flow from one tank to another at a higher level we have to use a pump. Water will not, of its own accord, flow uphill.

As we have already seen that heat will not, of its own accord, flow from a cold to a hot substance, some device is required if this has to be done. The device, which was suggested by Lord Kelvin about a century ago, is called a *heat pump*.

A refrigerator is a heat pump, as it transfers heat from inside a box to the atmosphere outside the box where the temperature is higher. To do this energy must be provided. The heat transferred, however, can be much greater than the electrical energy used to operate the motor. It would seem that we get more (heat) energy out than the (electrical) energy put in! *Can you explain this?* (50)

Heat pumps are now used to heat many buildings. The Royal Festival Hall in London is heated by extracting heat from the River Thames. In effect the freezing compartment of a refrigerator is in the river and the heat exchanger is inside the hall. Although this means that the river is being cooled all the time the amount of heat taken from it is so small that its effect on the river's temperature is negligible.

Small heat pumps for heating houses take heat from the ground outside the house. At present such schemes are expensive to install but they are likely to become more popular as costs drop.

Problem 51. If ammonia is vaporised in order to freeze an ice rink, find how much water at 0°C is frozen for every gram of ammonia vaporised.

If 10 kilograms of ammonia circulate through the cooling system every 5 minutes, how long will it take to freeze 500 kilograms of water at 0°C? (Latent heat of fusion of ice = 3·34 × 10⁵ J/kg and latent heat of vaporisation of ammonia = 1·34 × 10⁶ J/kg.)

Model Making

CHAPTER 12

Kinetic Theory

Daniel Bernoulli (1700–1782) imagined a gas to be made up of millions of tiny elastic particles flying around in all directions at high speeds. It was not until many years later, in 1827, that the Scottish botanist, Robert Brown, observed pollen grains in continuous motion in a liquid. Earlier in this course you saw smoke particles being jostled around in air. This is called *Brownian motion. Can you explain why Brownian motion suggests the existence of moving molecules?* (1) Here are two demonstrations to illustrate the kinetic model of a gas.

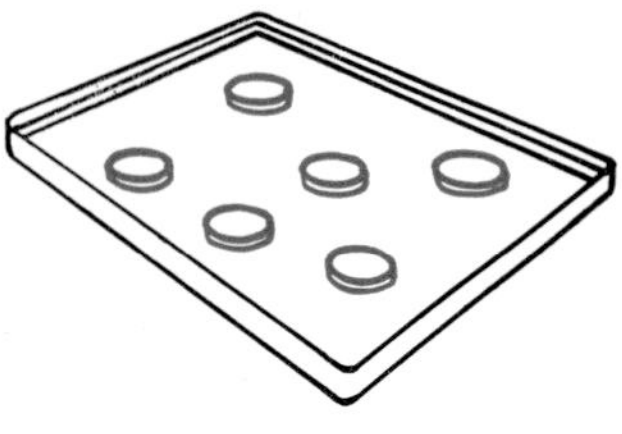

Model 12.1. Fix a strip of Eclipse magnetic rubber round the edge of a glass plate. Glue lids on top of a number of ring magnets (from old TV sets) and float them on carbon dioxide in the middle of the plate. It is important to make sure that the magnets have the same pole uppermost (Fig. 258).

Push a few of the floating magnets and watch the result. Do the floating magnets exert any force on the magnetic rubber strip? Why do they eventually come to rest?

Demonstration 12.2. Use an Advance vibrator[13] or an electric motor fitted with an eccentric[3] to power a kinetic model[3] as shown in Fig. 259. With only a few nickel spheres in the tube drop in a paper piston and watch what happens.

Repeat the experiment with twice as many spheres in the tube. What difference does this make to the piston? This corresponds to increasing the *density* of the gas.

What happens when the power to the vibrator is increased, that is, the spheres are given more energy? This corresponds to increasing the temperature of the gas, that is, the kinetic energy of the molecules.

If this is a good model of a gas, what would you expect to happen (a) when the density of a gas is increased (for example, by reducing the volume of a certain mass) and (b) when the temperature of a gas is increased? (2) *What experiments have you conducted which support this theory?* (3)

Let us now see if we can use our knowledge of Newtonian mechanics to calculate the force and hence the pressure which these molecules exert. *If they collide with the container elastically, will they exert more or less force than if they collide inelastically?* (4) *Why?* (5)

Demonstration 12.3. Place a steel block on a compression balance and drop (say) a cricket ball on to the block from a height of 1 metre. What is the maximum reading obtained? (A maximum reading

Fig. 258

Fig. 259

156

maximum
reading
device

Fig. 260

device is described in S.S.R. 152.) Now drop, from the same height, a ball of plasticine which has the same mass as the cricket ball (Fig. 260). Is the maximum reading greater or less than before? Does this agree with your reasoning?

Problem 6. *A man fires a spherical bullet (of mass 0·01 kg) at a steel wall (2 m × 2 m) as shown in Fig. 261. If the bullet bounces back at the same speed (500 m/s), find (a) the momentum of the*

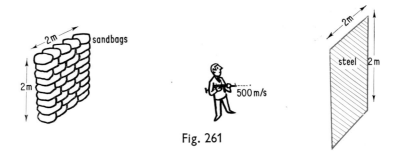

Fig. 261

bullet before it strikes the wall, (b) the momentum of the bullet after it strikes the wall, and (c) the change *in momentum of the bullet. Remember that momentum is a vector quantity. (d) If the bullet misses the man on its return journey and comes to rest embedded in a wall of sandbags (also 2 m × 2 m), what is the change of momentum of the bullet?*

Imagine now that a continuous stream of bullets is fired from the gun at a rate of 20 per second. Find (e) the total change of momentum of the bullets at the steel wall every second.

Now as

$$F = ma$$

$$= m\frac{\Delta v}{\Delta t}$$

$$= \frac{\Delta mv}{\Delta t}$$

you can find the average force exerted on the steel wall. It is the rate of change of momentum.

(f) From the force you can find the average pressure (force/area). What is the average pressure exerted on the steel wall?

(g) What is the pressure exerted on the wall of sandbags?

Suppose, Assume, Pretend

This title suggests a journey into the land of make-believe rather than an adventure in science. We are forever being told, usually by non-scientists, that 'science deals with facts' and now we are confronted with an invitation to exercise our imagination. The greatest scientists have had the greatest imaginations!

We are going to try to build a theory or model of a gas. Real gases are extremely complicated, particularly when they have molecules consisting of a number of different atoms. So we will simplify (and of course, let's face it, falsify) the picture in order to try to construct some kind of theory.

In this discussion we will not use any particular *units* as we are not expecting to obtain a numerical result. SI units could have been used throughout.

Imagine that a rectangular box of length *l*, breadth *b* and height *h*, contains molecules flying around in all directions. We will assume that on the average as many fly up and down (direction *h*) as in and out (direction *b*) or to and fro (direction *l*) (Fig. 262).

Let us imagine that the molecules are extremely small compared to the spaces between them and that they do not exert any force on one another except when they collide with each other or with the container. We will think of all such collisions as elastic so that no energy is lost.

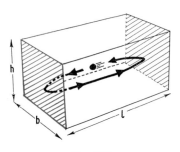

Fig. 262

To calculate the pressure exerted on the container by this gas we will start by thinking about a single molecule moving to and fro between the shaded walls (Fig. 262). If it moves with a constant speed *v* and takes a time Δt to move from one wall to the other and back again, then

$$v = \frac{\text{distance}}{\text{time}} = \frac{2l}{\Delta t}$$

Therefore

$$\Delta t = \frac{2l}{v}$$

As the molecule moves towards the red wall its momentum is *mv*, and as it leaves its momentum will be $-mv$, so that the

$$\text{change of momentum} = mv - (-mv)$$

$$= 2mv$$

As in the example of the bullet striking the steel wall the average force is equal to the rate of change of momentum (i.e. change of momentum per unit time)

$$F = \frac{\Delta mv}{\Delta t}$$

$$= \frac{2mv}{2l/v}$$

$$= \frac{2mv}{2l} \times v$$

Therefore

$$F = \frac{mv^2}{l}$$

Now let us imagine that there are *n* molecules in the box and that each has the same velocity *v*. On the average $\frac{1}{3}n$ molecules would be moving up and down, $\frac{1}{3}n$ in and out, and $\frac{1}{3}n$ to and fro between the shaded walls. The *total* force exerted on the red wall would therefore be

$$F = \tfrac{1}{3}n\frac{mv^2}{l}$$

and the average pressure p would be

$$p = \frac{\text{force}}{\text{area}}$$

$$= \frac{\frac{1}{3}n\dfrac{mv^2}{l}}{b \times h}$$

$$= \tfrac{1}{3}\frac{nmv^2}{lbh}$$

but $\qquad lbh = $ the volume (V) of our box so

$$p = \tfrac{1}{3}\frac{nmv^2}{V}$$

or $\qquad pV = \tfrac{1}{3}nmv^2$

The gas molecules are flying hither and thither at random. As they are colliding with each other and the walls millions of times a second, their speeds will be varying all the time. Our assumption, then, that all their speeds were the same is hardly likely to be correct. If, however, we take the average value of all the individual values of v^2, we should get the same result. We will write this average value as $\overline{v^2}$. It is called 'v^2 bar'. Our equation can then be written as

$$pV = \tfrac{1}{3}nm\overline{v^2}$$

As we know that the kinetic energy of a moving body is $\tfrac{1}{2}mv^2$ we could rewrite this equation as

$$pV = \tfrac{2}{3}n\left(\tfrac{1}{2}m\overline{v^2}\right)$$

where the expression in the bracket $(\tfrac{1}{2}m\overline{v^2})$ represents the average kinetic energy of a molecule. This assumes that all the kinetic energy is due to the molecules moving from place to place, and ignores any kinetic energy due to their tumbling head over heels or vibrating as they go. The total kinetic energy of all the molecules is therefore $n(\tfrac{1}{2}m\overline{v^2})$, so that

$$pV = \tfrac{2}{3} \times \text{ kinetic energy}$$

If the kinetic energy of the molecules depends on the temperature, we can say that when the temperature is constant the kinetic energy is constant, or

$$pV = \text{ constant at constant temperature}$$

Let us see if this prediction, from our simple theory, is supported by experiment.

Experiment 12.4. Take a length of Vinyl tubing$_{12}$ (Portland N.T.5) and attach it to a $100\ \text{cm}^3$ syringe$_{16}$ (Fig. 263). Coat the plunger with oil to make it airtight. Pour mercury into the tube until the longer limb is full, and then clamp it. Move the piston until the syringe contains $60\ \text{cm}^3$ of air, and adjust the level of the syringe to reduce to a minimum the amount of air in the Vinyl tubing. Why?

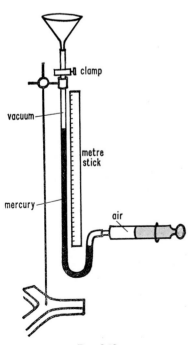

clamp

vacuum

metre stick

mercury

air

Fig. 263

Fig. 264

Measure the pressure of the air in the syringe in centimetres of mercury.

Repeat this experiment with 40, 50, 70 and 80 cm³ of air in the syringe, and plot graphs showing the air pressure against volume and against 1/volume. Calculate the product pV for each result. What do you conclude?

Demonstration 12.5. An alternative demonstration utilises a Bourdon pressure gauge₃ to measure the pressure of air above oil in a glass tube. The volume of the air can be read directly on the tube. Why does the pressure gauge never read zero? (Fig. 264).

From the readings you obtain plot graphs of pressure against volume and against 1/volume. Calculate the product pV for each result. What do you conclude?

Similar equipment using a mercury thread is also available commercially₉.

The results you have just obtained were originally found by Robert Boyle (1627–1691) and are usually referred to as *Boyle's Law*. It states that *for a given mass of gas at constant temperature the pressure is inversely proportional to the volume.*

Do the results of the last experiment support our kinetic theory of gases? (7)

What would a graph of pressure/density for a given mass of gas look like? (8)

The results of Boyle's Law can be written

$$pV = \text{constant } (k)$$

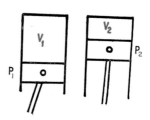

$$p_1 V_1 = k = p_2 V_2$$
$$\therefore \quad p_1 V_1 = p_2 V_2$$

where p_1 is the original pressure of a gas
V_1 is the original volume of the gas
p_2 is the final pressure of the gas
V_2 is the final volume of the gas

Problems

9. *100 cm³ of air at atmospheric pressure (10^5 N/m²) is contained in a syringe. If the volume is reduced to (a) 50 cm³ (b) 20 cm³ what will be the new pressure if the temperature does not change?*

10. *If the piston in a cylinder containing 300 cm³ of gas at atmospheric pressure (10^5 N/m²) moves outwards so that the pressure falls to 8×10^4 N/m², find the volume of the gas if the temperature remains constant.*

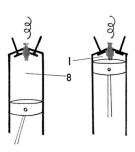

Fig. 266

11. *The compression ratio of a car engine is the volume of gas in the cylinder when the piston is at the bottom divided by the volume when it is at the top of its stroke. If the compression ratio of an engine is 8:1, how will the pressure when the piston is at the top compare with the pressure when the piston is at the bottom of its stroke?* (*Fig. 266*). *Assume the gas is not ignited and that the temperature has not changed.*

Kinetic Energy and Temperature

Let us return to our ideal gas in which all the (heat) energy is translational kinetic energy, i.e. the energy of the molecules moving from place to place. Gases such as helium with one-atom molecules are very near to this 'ideal'.

As the kinetic energy of the molecules increases with temperature we might guess that the kinetic energy is proportional to the absolute temperature; that is, kinetic energy $= cT$ (where c is a constant).

From page 159 we have

$$pV = \tfrac{2}{3} \times \text{kinetic energy}$$

Therefore $pV = \tfrac{2}{3}cT$

,, $\dfrac{pV}{T} = \tfrac{2}{3}c$ which is a constant

,, $\dfrac{pV}{T} = \text{constant}$

We have already discovered with our gas thermometer (page 121) that

$$\frac{p}{T} = \text{constant}$$

for a constant volume of gas, and this simple kinetic theory agrees with this experimental result. We will now consider the change of volume with temperature.

Experiment 12.6. (*a*) Dry the air in a 30 or 50 cm³ syringe₁₆ by placing it in boiling brine or by putting a little phosphorous pentoxide inside the syringe. Lubricate the syringe with silicone fluid₁₇ (MS 510/5000cS).

Push a piece of rubber tubing over the Luer mount and clamp it so that it is airtight. The air inside will be maintained at atmospheric pressure as the plunger is free to move (Fig. 267).

Now place the syringe in water and note the volume of the air at various temperatures between 100°C and 0°C. Finally place the syringe in a mixture of methylated spirits and dry ice to give a temperature of −72°C. Plot a graph showing the variation of volume with temperature.

If the volume variation continued in the same way until it was zero, what would be the temperature of zero volume?

(*b*) An alternative method uses a bead of mercury in a capillary tube sealed at one end. The volume is then proportional to the length of the column of air.

Fig. 267

Calculate one or two values of $\frac{V}{T}$ from the results of the last experiment, assuming absolute zero to be $-273°C$ ($0°K$). *Do your results support the kinetic theory?* (12) This relationship is known either as Charles' Law or Gay-Lussac's Law after the French scientists who discovered it about 1787. It states that **the volume of a given mass of gas at constant pressure is directly proportional to the absolute temperature.**

The Gas Equation

From our simplified kinetic theory of gases we arrived at

$$\frac{pV}{T} = \text{constant}$$

Although this relationship was obtained for an ideal gas with one-atom molecules, the results of three experiments have shown that this relationship holds reasonably well for dry air over a range of pressures near atmospheric pressure. Many other more accurate experiments have shown that this equation is only approximately correct. Nevertheless, we can, within limits, make predictions about real gases, particularly the so-called permanent gases, using the relationship

$$\frac{p_1 V_1}{T_1} = \frac{p_2 V_2}{T_2}$$

This is called the *gas equation.*

Summary of Gas Laws

1. Boyle's Law: $pV = \text{constant}$ (temperature kept constant).

2. Charles' or Gay-Lussac's Law: $\frac{V}{T} = \text{constant}$ (pressure kept constant.)

3. Pressure Law: $\frac{p}{T} = \text{constant}$ (volume kept constant).

All these can be summarised by

$$\frac{pV}{T} = \text{constant}$$

Project 12.7. Connect a large and a small syringe as shown in Fig. 268. Lubricate the pistons and load them until they balance. Find the total weight (load + piston) and hence the pressure on each side. Explain your results in terms of the kinetic theory of gases.

Project 12.8. Dip a tumbler in hot soapy water, take it out, turn it upside down and place the empty tumbler on a sloping sheet of glass (for example, a mirror). Explain what happens.

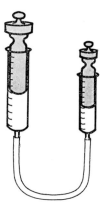

Fig. 268

Problems

13. *Explain in terms of the kinetic theory why a paper pellet can be fired from a bicycle pump.*

14. *Explain in terms of the kinetic theory why the pressure of a gas increases as the temperature rises.*

15. *If the average speed of hydrogen molecules at room temperature and atmospheric pressure is about 1 mile per second, what would be their average speed if the temperature remained the same and the pressure was doubled?*

16. *In a mixture of hydrogen and oxygen gases at the same temperature which molecules would move faster? Why?*

17. *Will the pressure in a car tyre be greater or less after a long fast journey? Why?*

18. *In the simple kinetic theory given above we ignored the attraction between the molecules of gas. Do you think such attractive forces in a real gas would cause the actual pressure to be greater or less than the predicted pressure?*

19. *Discuss each of the following in terms of the kinetic or molecular theory of matter.*

(a) *The three states of matter.*

(b) *The pressure of a gas.*

(c) *Expansion of a gas with rise of temperature.*

(d) *Latent heat.*

20. *If your gas-meter measures the volume of gas flowing per second do you or the Gas Board profit when the gas pressure is low? Explain your answer.*

21. *If a cricket ball strikes (a) a stationary bat (b) a bat moving towards it (c) a bat moving away from it, how will the speed at which the ball rebounds be affected? If molecules behaved in the same way what would be the effect of compressing a gas?*

22. *A certain mass of oxygen has a volume of 5 m³ at 27°C. If the pressure remains the same, what will be its volume at 77°C?*

23. *At an altitude of 5·5 km (18,000 feet) the atmospheric pressure is about 5×10^4 N/m², that is, about half of the pressure at sea-level. If 1 kg of air has a volume of 0·8 m³ at sea-level, what will be its volume at an altitude of 5·5 km? State the density of air at those two levels, assuming the temperature remains the same.*

24. *Assuming that a man has to obtain the same mass of oxygen every second at different levels, how would his rate of breathing be affected by his altitude?*

25. *A water barometer stands at 10 metres. If an air bubble has a volume of 0·3 cm³ at a depth of 10 metres below the surface of a pond, what will be its volume if it rises to the surface?*

26. *If 50 cm³ of oxygen is collected at 17°C and at a pressure of 74 cm Hg, find its volume at s.t.p. (that is, 0°C and 76 cmHg).*

27. *When a motorist says his tyre pressure is 30 lbf/in² he means 30 lbf/in² in excess of atmospheric pressure, so that if the atmospheric pressure is 15 lbf/in² the tyre pressure is 45 lbf/in². How will the density of air in a tyre at this pressure compare with its density at normal atmospheric pressure?*

28. *An under-sea house is at a depth of 20·6 metres below the surface. Find the air pressure in the house, assuming normal*

atmospheric pressure to be $10^5 N/m^2$, which is equivalent to 10.3 metres of water.

29. The density of air at s.t.p. is about 1.2 kg/m^3 and of liquid air 900 kg/m^3. What do these figures tell you about the spacing of the molecules in the two states?

Visual Aids

16 mm Films: Gas pressure and Molecular collisions.$_{26}$ 2D.3000.
Molecular Motions$_{26}$ 2DC.2998.
Behaviour of Gases (P.S.S.C.)$_{26}$ 2D.2637.

Suppliers

1. I.M.O. (Electronics) Ltd., 313 Edgware Road, London W.2.
2. Venner Ltd., Kingston By-pass, New Malden, Surrey.
3. Philip Harris Ltd., 63 Ludgate Hill, Birmingham W.3.
4. W. B. Nicolson Ltd., Thornliebank Industrial Estate, Glasgow.
5. Dawe Instruments Ltd., Western Avenue, Acton, London W.3.
6. Rollo Industries Ltd., St. Andrew's Works, Bonnybridge, Stirlingshire.
7. Dexion Ltd., Empire Way, Wembley Park, Middlesex.
8. Panax Equipment Ltd., Holmethorpe Industrial Estate, Redhill, Surrey.
9. Griffin & George Ltd., Braeview Park, Nerston, East Kilbride, Lanarkshire.
10. Serinco, 6 Swan Place, Glenrothes, Fife.
11. Polaroid Ltd., Queensway House, Queensway, Hatfield, Herts.
12. A. H. Baird Ltd., 33–39 Lothian Street, Edinburgh 1.
13. Advance Components Ltd., Roebuck Road, Hainault, Ilford, Essex.
14. Educational Measurements Ltd., 1 Brook Avenue, Warsash, Southampton.
15. Donray Models, 302 Morningside Road, Edinburgh 10.
16. Hospital & Laboratory Supplies Ltd., 12 Charterhouse Square, London E.C.1.
17. Hopkin & Williams Ltd., Freshwater Road, Chadwell Heath, Essex.
18. Ealing Scientific Ltd., 23 Leman Street, London E.1.
19. Electronic Applications (Commercial) Ltd., Endeavour House, North Circular Road, London N.W.2.
20. Morris Laboratory Instruments (Sales) Ltd., 96/98 High Street, Putney, London S.W.15.
21. Dunlop Rubber Co. Ltd., Education Section, 10/12 King Street, St James's, London S.W.1.
22. Visual Publications Ltd., 197 Kensington High Street, London W.8.
23. Rank Film Library, 1 Aintree Road, Perivale, Greenford, Middlesex.
24. Educational Productions Ltd., East Ardsley, Wakefield, Yorkshire.
25. Petroleum Films Bureau, 4 Brook Street, Hanover Square, London W.1.
26. Scottish Central Film Library, 16/17 Woodside Terrace, Charing Cross, Glasgow C.3.
27. Gas Council Film Library, 1 Grosvenor Place, London S.W.1.
28. Esso Petroleum Co. Ltd., Public Relations Department, Victoria Street, London S.W.1.

Index